✳✳✳

The Inner Path
from Where You Are
to Where
You Want to Be

✳✳✳

Other books by Terry Cole-Whittaker

WHAT YOU THINK OF ME IS NONE OF MY BUSINESS
HOW TO HAVE MORE IN A HAVE-NOT WORLD

The Inner Path
from Where You Are
to Where
You Want to Be

TERRY COLE-WHITTAKER

RAWSON ASSOCIATES : *New York*

Library of Congress Cataloging-in-Publication Data

Cole-Whittaker, Terry, 1939–
The inner path from where you are to where you
want to be.

1. Spiritual life. 2. Cole-Whittaker, Terry,
1939–   . I. Title.
BL624.C64   1986   291.4'4   84-42930
ISBN 0-89256-283-8

Packaged by Rapid Transcript, a division of March Tenth, Inc.
Composition by Folio Graphics Company, Inc.
Manufactured by Fairfield Graphics, Fairfield, Pennsylvania
Designed by Jacques Chazaud
Published simultaneously in Canada by Collier Macmillan Canada, Inc.
First Edition

Friendship and partnership are what allow us to engage in the kind of interaction that stirs up our deepest hidden feelings, thoughts, beliefs, and fears and then inspires us to greater heights of love, sharing, play, truth, and commitment. The people in my life have always given me the opportunity to become what I am because of their willingness to engage in the relationship 100 percent.

I dedicate this book to my friend Robert Northrop, whose love, support, and playful nature pulled me through much-needed lessons to a greater love and appreciation of both myself and others.

I also dedicate this book to Reuben Zeigler, who set me free into the realm of eternal life and returned me to my child self. His love and devotion to his own spirituality beyond the material world inspired me in my eternal quest, and thereby I was born freely into life.

Contents

Preface

Over the eighteen months spanning 1984 and the first half of 1985 I made major changes in my life because of a profound spiritual awakening. This awakening has affected every area of my life, especially my role as a minister with Terry Cole-Whittaker Ministries. I am very excited about the new direction in my life, which has produced a 180-degree turn for me, from the outer path to the inner path.

I know that many of you are going through great changes, too. Like me, you are facing choices involving the call of the heart and the call of the world. I know that you are, as I am, having to trust your feelings, your intuition, and yourself as never before. I also know that no matter what anyone thinks, you have to do what you must do.

For me, the making of these choices has produced an immense shift in focus. Where before I felt called upon to share a message with the world, I now feel called to share only with those who are truly interested and with whom I share a common vision. What is occurring in me now is beyond my greatest expectations. When I started down this path, I had no idea what awaited me around the next corner. My actions may have shocked many people, especially those who have participated in my ministry either at close range or from a distance, whether by telephone or through the mail. It was never my intention to abandon anyone or to invalidate any teaching. In fact, what has happened is the *result* of the teaching—*I trusted my inner guidance.*

I have written this book to explain how and why my ministry was dissolved and to reveal some of the exciting experiments in life and living that I am now undertaking.

The age in which we live is a time of great spiritual awakening for all people. Each person awakens at his own rate, but the overall process has begun to pick up speed, and I am sure you, too, are seeing this all around you. It is no longer a time for segregated and dogmatic religious organizations, no longer a time for ministers and congregation to have separate identities. It is time instead for them to join together as one. This is one of the reasons why I dissolved the organization surrounding my ministry. It seemed unnatural to me.

The major focus of my work now will be through a much smaller, far less structured, and totally educational organization called the Foundation for Spiritual Study. Through the Foundation I will offer programs for any and all persons committed to the same search to which I am committed: the search for individual truth, not truth by acclamation.

The work of the Foundation will be to bring people together, not to hear teachings, but to share the *experience of the search*, outpourings of the heart, confidences of the soul.

This book is such a sharing. It is an outpouring of the heart and a confidence of the soul. It may and it may not benefit anyone. All of us can be inspired by others—you can be inspired by me and I can be inspired by you—but ultimately we each have to be our own ideal and find our own truth. However, if you have embarked on a journey toward your own understandings and your individual truth and would like some company along the way, I think you will enjoy this book, for you and I are walking the same path.

Love,

Terry

Acknowledgments

The acknowledgments in my first two books still hold true for me today. I am what I am because of courageous individuals who dare to risk, who go beyond the imagined boundaries of conformity and thus pave the way for others so that we may all be released into the light. I am eternally grateful to the pioneers, explorers, experimenters, and adventurers who reach out into the unknown, who test the waters, who ask the unaskable questions, who dare to push toward the outer and inner limits of our consciousness and physical universe.

I salute those who are willing to learn from their mistakes, who get back up and run full steam ahead into life even after a bad experience, no matter whether others were there to support them or not. I know what you are up to!

I acknowledge everyone who, in having the courage to trust him- or herself, inspired another also to believe in the inherent goodness and purity of all life.

Thank you, Eleanor and Ken Rawson, Elizabeth Backman, Cheryl Rosoff, Ollie Hesketh, Roger Lane, Sandy Scott, Dick Circuit, Ed Blitz, Robert Pante, Steve Zack, Sonia Powers, and my entire staff.

An extra special thank-you to my friend of the soul, Neale Marshall-Walsch, truly a master writer and editor, who always brings his Higher Self to the challenge of producing a book and in so doing inspires me to new levels of sharing and creation.

And thanks to all of you who will share this book with me. I bless you in my heart and I love you.

The Inner Path
from Where You Are
to Where
You Want to Be

1. The Beginning
of the End . . .
and the End of
the Beginning

When the Holy One created the world He
engraved the Mystery of Faith in letters of
sparkling light; He engraved it above and below,
because it is the same Mystery and because the
world below is the mirror of that which is above.

The Holy Kabbalah
Book V, No. V

This is a book for masters. This is not a book for those who still try to live up to someone else's ideal. It is not for those who give their lives to someone else. There are plenty of books for those people, and there is nothing *wrong* with those people. They are where they should be, in their perfect place. However, I am only writing for those who are in a different place, a place at the very cutting edge of their own higher understanding. This book is for people who dare to move on even from there but may need a friend along the way to listen and respond with love when they ask, "Is what I'm feeling all right? Is what I'm being called to do going to work? Am I going to lose it all?"

This book is for those who have found something greater than anything they ever experienced before and want more of it. They have had a taste of the cosmic, they have had a taste of the unseen, they have had a taste of who they can be. This is for those who would be the masters of their bodies, of their feelings, of life itself, who want to take their place with the ascended masters of all time.

If this does not sound like you, this book is not for you. You may even ridicule it and say that it makes no sense. That, of course, will be true. This book is not about making sense. It is not about being reasonable. There is nothing reasonable about this book, so if you're looking for a reasonable book, put it down right now. But while you're about it, take a look at how far "being reasonable" has taken you in your life.

If you don't understand this book, it may not be your time. But then, perhaps you need to open yourself in a way you haven't known before and *make* it your time—your time to confront the next step, your time to move to the next level, your time to be who you really are.

I am committed to the Divine Experiment, and I see that I have been all my life. I also see that for any of us to become a master, it takes an act of will. In our day-to-day activities, we must call forth the wisdom, the love, the strength, and the energy we possess within ourselves to deal with the issues of life from an enlightened perspective. You become what you are only by what you bring forth from yourself in day-to-day, person-to-person encounters. Great masters throughout history—those we call geniuses and extraordinary—are, at their core, the same as everyone else. What separates them is that they had the courage to step out, make a demand upon themselves, and draw out divine knowing, wisdom, joy, and love.

• • •

I am no longer a minister. I used to be, but I am not any more. I presented my last church service on Easter Sunday, 1985. I know I shocked a lot of people when I abruptly announced my retirement from religion in what many thought was a spontaneous decision. It was not. The decision was four years in the making.

I did not leave religion because I no longer love God. I love God now more than ever, and I am grateful to all spiritual warriors and all spiritual masters, especially Jesus the Christ, for what they brought to me and what they awakened in me. Yet I know now that it is never any person, but the energy and the essence they bring that calls forth a corresponding vibration within others. I didn't know this three years ago. I'm not the same person today that I was then.

I was a minister for thirteen years. I started a television ministry eight years ago, and what I know now I didn't know then. Religion was a wonderful boat to get me from one shore to another, but it is important to get out of the boat when you reach the other side. And that's exactly what I have done. I got out because religion is a system, and because any kind of system, whether it be religious, political, economic, social, or philosophical, has inherent in it an enslaving requirement for unquestioning adherence to that particular doctrine, theory, or dogma. This is true because systems by their nature must be self-perpetuating or they cease to exist.

Systems operate at every level of life. There are family systems, community systems, national and world systems. Obviously, there is even a universal system—that by which the universe runs and, say some, by which it was created. I am among those who believe that the secret of life is found in this universal system—not just the secret of life's beginning but of life as it continues through each new moment. It is when people move beyond the world's systems of thought into the universal system that they begin to leave many of their neighbors behind.

Systems work for us because we must lead our lives in some kind of structured form. We search for shape and direction. There was no shape and direction when we began, but we found that didn't work because we couldn't know ourselves. That's why we invented systems in the first place.

In our cosmic relationship with one another we express life by agreement. We have to do this or there would be sheer chaos. So there will always be agreements in your experience, agreements that you have with others and with life itself. Out of these agreements inevitably spring systems of thought about what controls and even creates your daily experience.

The agreements by which you live change as you become enlightened—aware—and therein lies the problem. As those points on which you agree with others become fewer, the system that you and others have constructed together becomes less and less useful to you.

You have undoubtedly experienced this already to an extent. As you have become more enlightened, more aware and more conscious of your Self, you have no doubt noticed yourself becoming a more loving and more secure being. You have become more trusting—trusting in yourself, trusting in God, trusting in Nature, and trusting in your own feelings and intuition. You need the structures of the world system less and less.

This is exactly what happened to me and this is what caused me ultimately to dissolve Terry Cole-Whittaker Ministries, abandon the system of religion, and move into a more direct experience of who I am, without the need or use of systems of any kind.

The Change and How It Began

This movement or shift, which changed my whole life, started for me during the early part of 1981, before I met my fourth husband. Since then everything about me has changed. I was wearing designer clothes, designer suits, high heels, tight panty hose, jewelry, things that were tight around my waist and cut off my circulation and my energy, because that was what looked successful. Now that I've really begun to experience the joy of my own being, I ask myself why I should sacrifice my comfort so that someone else can think I am "making it."

We all ask ourselves such questions sooner or later, and when we hear no answer we begin to see the insanity of the world enslavement program. I participated in that program, and I got out of it only by going fully into it. I went fully into the world system of Success, Fame, Fortune, and Power. As a woman, it was particularly significant and important to me to do this.

I remember feeling like a second class citizen because I was a woman yet knowing in my heart that I was first class. I was subject to the male domination syndrome and as a woman was not thought of—by others or by myself—as an equal. I thought that the way to gain my independence was to win at the male game, which I did.

There could hardly have been a better place for me to play and win than in a church. Religion, in particular, has always been considered a male domain.

Religion, of course, is what started the whole enslavement program to begin with. It first began when one god convinced another that he was better and that, since he was better, he had more power and could put a curse on the other. The one who was cursed began to believe he was lesser, and in that moment the enslavement program began. Later, "in the name of God," priests became the instruments of enslavement, the damners and the savers.

From that system came other worldly systems of people who were *better than* and people who were *lesser than*. From that system came the royalty game, the games of government and business, and all other enslavement programs wherein one person or class becomes king of the mountain. Women were less than second class, yet, interestingly, men were thought to get their souls from the female. The female was to depend on the male for her life support, because her purpose was to bear the children of the planet and she could not carry on the lineage—she could not be true to her feminine, creative nature—if she were not protected and taken care of.

From that time to this men have been afraid of women, because without women the race would be lost, and women have been angry with men, because if men ceased to "provide," women could not do what they were intended to do. Women therefore felt subservient and dependent.

What I Had to Start . . . and Why I Had to Stop

In order for me, in the body of a woman, to become the master that I choose to be, I went into the male-dominated system, or game, of religion for myself. I did it because I asked myself, If a woman is to become a master, what better place is there than that which deals with God, with the Universal Power, with the Creator of All? And what better way for her than to become the head of her own church?

I did exactly that. I don't think I did it with conscious forethought; I did not know when I started that I would one day create my own church, really my own denomination. In those days I was not consciously choosing as I am now; that's just the way things evolved. I know now that nothing evolves without the active decision of the evolver, which I was. Actually, I chose it all.

I soon had a fast-growing following comprised of those who had the same need and the same desire to break away from orthodoxy. There must be a lot of us in the world. When I assumed my first full-time ministerial position, we started with fifty people in the congregation of a church I took over in La Jolla, California. Within three years we had grown to over five thousand. Then we went on television and grew to what some claim to have been over 2 million. (Obviously, the actual numbers don't matter.) We were on fourteen television stations reaching 250 or more cities at one juncture, including Los Angeles, New York, San Francisco, and points north, south, east, and west. The papers were describing us as the "fastest growing television ministry in America," and I was being called, of all things, "the high priestess of yuppiedom."

Our ministry appealed to people who were stepping out beyond the world enslavement game. It was popular with people from all walks of life, from every social strata and with every conceivable prior religious conviction and training. It cut across all boundaries, and it melted every barrier precisely because its message had neither boundary nor barrier, emphasizing life and love without limitation.

To say that the ministry was a success, to say that I had my dream come true, would be the understatement of the decade. In going into the system of religion, I succeeded beyond my wildest expectation. I had all this and could have had more.

In the position I was in, I could have kept going. I would have had more followers, I would have had a bigger organization, I would have had my *own religion*. Yet today my ministry is no more.

Why?

That is the question many people who gave their hearts and souls to this ministry have been asking. It is a question many others, including those connected with us in but the most peripheral ways, wanted answered in those first few weeks after Easter 1985, when I told my congregation that I was stepping down. In this book you will find the answer.

Why, then, do I say this is a book for masters? Because it is more than my story of how a ministry was born, grew, and came to its natural conclusion. It is instead the sharing of a journey, a personal odyssey from spiritual imprisonment to spiritual liberation, and what made such a great escape possible. It is a revelation of the secret of that escape, an escape from a system of enslavement within which so many have been caught. And finally, it is a revelation of ways to *remain* free. Those who have undertaken the same journey will understand. Those who have walked the same path will know whereof I speak.

10

To them I offer this book as a gift of love and friendship. With it I extend the hand of companionship, a companionship of the heart, mind, and soul. This book is for practicing masters, and if you are a master practicing, you will understand perfectly why it was written.

We teach what we choose to learn.

2. When the Transition Began

Terry Cole-Whittaker Ministries came to an end when a phase of my life came to an end. That phase was a transition period that lasted four years, beginning in the early part of 1981. It reached its conclusion on Easter Sunday, 1985, when more than five thousand people came together at the San Diego Performing Arts Center to celebrate with us not only the resurrection of Jesus Christ but the eternal resurrection of the human spirit. For me, and for all of us in that huge hall that Easter, it was a day of poignant emotion, and so it was life at its best.

The ministry, which each of those five thousand people had supported with their participation, love, and contributions, was presenting its last service. Those five thousand people, all of whom had been nourished by the ministry, came to be nourished again one last time. They came to rejoice and share the energy that had played such an integral part in creating our organization; they came prepared to use that powerful energy to push on to the next level of experience in their individual and collective spiritual lives.

It had taken three weeks for all of us to get over the shock of the first announcement of the ministry's dissolution. Even though I made that announcement, I was as much in shock as anyone else, not because I was surprised by the content of the announcement—the decision, as I've said, was actually four years in the making, and so I certainly did not surprise myself with it—but because of the timing and the manner in which the announcement itself was made. And that is to say nothing of the reaction to it.

It was March 17, St. Patrick's Day, and the luck o' the Irish had to have been with me, for it was on that morning that I faced the biggest monster in the universe in a life and death battle—and won. The monster, of course, was the demon of indecision. I had long before realized that I no longer wished to be doing what I was doing. I had long ago achieved what I needed to achieve. I had become a powerful, prosperous, and well-known woman who had succeeded at a man's game. I had freed myself from the concern of what people think. I had freed myself from concern about what other religious leaders would say. I had freed myself from concern about what successful men might say. And I had freed myself from concern about what women might say. I *became myself*; I used the system to transcend the system.

Of course, all of those previous concerns were my own projections, plus the fears I made up. I had met the challenge I had created for myself so that I *could* wake up and see the light. It wasn't a case of giving up everything I loved; it was a case of ending what did not bring me happiness and peace. In life, you must be willing to do whatever it takes to find and be yourself. *You are all you have.* In expressing your courage to be you, you provide others the courage to be themselves. Systems that once served you can become prisons of the spirit. It's okay if you want to be part of "the system." I no longer could.

To make matters worse, I had become bored with the system. I began to feel the pain of staying on top and defending my position and building a point of view and a philosophy. I realized that in creating a game that could be played outside the system, I had produced a *system of my own*!

Why "the System" Became Frightening

All systems are the creation of the person or people who establish them, yet frequently they are called God-ordained. And at one level that is so, because we are God and we made them up. At another level I kept telling people not to get caught up in my system, that I was no more right about anything than anyone else, but few listened to me. I stood behind the lectern and said, "I'm not 'it'; don't believe anything I say. Believe only what your heart says is true." But the more I said it, the more people believed me without hesitation. This was probably because, despite what I said, part of me wanted people to play my game and make my system theirs, in the name of making a difference.

The result of all this was that when I changed what I said because I'd learned something new and altered my own reality because of it, people would get nervous (some would actually become angry and upset) because something I said was different from what I'd said the week before. Of course it was different! *I* was different. I was speaking only for myself, yet others made my words their truth!

No one else's truth can be yours, although there are some simple general truths I have found: (1) You are *it*. (2) Through feeling, thought creates the outside world. (3) Because we all have free will, it is up to us to shape our own lives moment to moment.

As I began really to understand how the system I had created was working, I started to become frightened. What was I to do now? *I* could enslave people just as other systems had enslaved people! I could enslave them with the same religious thing about tithing—"give ten percent to the church"—that others had used. I knew that giving *worked* and that my life had come from contribution. Yet this was *my* truth, not theirs. I could tell people that I had the final word because I am the authority. I could become their guru, their "priestess," and even their ideal, to the extent that some would pattern their lives after me, adopting my values and practicing my virtues.

All of these things I could do, and they are the things people at the head of systems *must* do in order to keep their system going. This is what a pope must do, a rabbi must do, a Fidel Castro must do, a Ronald Reagan must do, because if they do not, the system disintegrates and the following they've collected disappears.

Unfortunately, many people become so trapped in religious guilt and fear and in the belief that the elite are better than they are that they give away their power. If you are a religious leader, they may give that power to you. You become the hero they worship and hate. They will hear what you tell them of your experience and, comparing themselves with you, see themselves as weak and helpless and hopeless. Then they will want someone to save them, and you will be elected. But no one ever loves or is grateful to a savior. So be your own ideal; *never desire to be another's.* Others, too, must become their own ideal.

You can only share *your* story, you can only share *your* truth, you can only share what works for you. Everyone out there has free will. Even surrendering to the will of God for your eternal joy, peace, and happiness requires that *you will it,* or it can't happen. It's always up to you. *Everything is always up to you.*

Many people today believe that Jesus will save them. These people are asleep and refuse to wake up from their belief that they are lesser, or inferior. They have not heard what Jesus had to say.

Jesus' entire message was that you are *not* less, but every time his words came to that, people turned them around and swore he meant something else. He said, "Why are you so amazed? These things and more shall you also do," but people didn't want to hear that. It had to be only *he* who could do these things. Otherwise who would save them? If there was no one person more powerful than the rest, if everyone's power was equal, *who would be responsible*? What would be your excuse and whom could you blame?

"Why am I?" "Who is God?" and "What's it all about?" are the questions every religion asks. It is only the answers that differ from religion to religion.

Some religions tell us that if you dare to ask forbidden questions or, worse yet, worship yourself and become your own ideal, hell will be your punishment, for this, they say, is blasphemy. To degrade yourself, to regard yourself as a worm in the dust, is considered the height of spirituality.

Yet the knowledge of who you are and of your divine connection with All That Is and the uplifting of yourself into the highest aspects of your being are the taste of heaven, the taste of bliss and joy, the pearl of great price. When this uplifting begins, everything else starts to fall apart. When everything you have been taught, have believed in or accepted as right, starts to lose its hold on you, then, quite literally, all hell breaks loose, and heaven has made its first appearance before you.

How the Shift Began

So it was in 1981, before meeting my fourth husband, that I began the movement and the shift which brought me to where I am now. I was already experiencing the first feelings of bliss. I was beginning to feel for the first time the joy of play, play just for the sheer delight of it, in my life, as well as satisfaction at being with myself, whether meditating, experiencing spiritual revelation, reading the words of Jesus in the Bible, or reading *A Course in Miracles*.

It is a biological truth that when you pull oxygen into your cells you begin to feel alive in your body and the pain begins to leave. Pain results from withholding love. It is what you feel when you "protect" yourself from God and the love that you are. I was already experiencing greater peace and pleasure in my body. I had been doing a lot of body work—Rolfing, Hellerwork—so that a lot of the pain in my body started giving way to bliss as I allowed myself more happiness. The pain of past trauma and emotional hurts was leaving, because as the present and future became more desirable, I no longer wished to stare into the past.

I was feeling that what I now wanted in a relationship was a spiritual equal, both a playmate and a friend. At the same time I was experiencing less and less interest in my organization. Its increased size and ambitions began to make my involvement with it more tedious, time-consuming, and difficult. No sooner would we meet one target or goal than we'd set another. No sooner would we "get there" than we'd change the "there" to which we were going.

I was part of this whole process, of course. One part of me was still caught up in the game of bigger-and-better even as another part of me was starting to rebel. And then the second part overcame the first. But the old fear kept coming up: What would I do if I disbanded the organization? This was all I knew! Where would I go? The age-old question "How can I do *only* what I *love to do and still make a living?"* kept coming up. I knew that the part of me caught up in the game of bigger-and-better wanted more in order to help me feel worthy and beautiful. But isn't that what everything is about? Did I need the organization or even a relationship for that?

Everything was there to serve me in obtaining more happiness. I was not missing anything. It was obvious what brought me happiness, and it was not the organization. It was the teaching. It was the personal sharing of life and how it is for me, which I notice I'm still doing in this book, still doing at lectures, programs, and special events, still doing at workshops and seminars. And I will probably keep sharing until . . . well, until I don't do it anymore!

During this time of transition I began to know that work in a corporate context wasn't for me. Going to work was stressful because I had to run an organization that had grown very rapidly. There were so many demands and departments and things to deal with that we were constantly behind; we were constantly making decisions at the last minute, and planning was unheard of. There were more and more people, more and more responsibilities. I felt the rush toward greater expansion conflicting with a desire to run away and be at peace. I knew that the organization *must* grow if we were to get the message out to more people, meet the overhead, and—most important—keep me doing what I loved: speaking and inspiring.

I wanted to be well known because I thought renown could help me reach more people and because I wanted to be accepted as an equal in the world. I wanted to know that I could stand there with the best of them, take my place as someone who made a difference. This was a wonderful calling. I had begun to see that if anybody could do anything, so could I; that no one is better than I am; that every dream and desire I had . . . well, I could fulfill them just like anyone else.

It was the desire to prove all this that kept me doing what I was doing, even though I *knew* that running a big organization wasn't it for me. Some of it I loved, but it created immense conflict. So when I met my fourth husband, I was ready to have a playmate, because I had noticed that when I had a playmate and a lover I could forget the job, be myself, and return to the feeling I had as a child—enjoy the freedom just to be, whether walking through the streets of Paris, surfing in Mexico, snorkling in Hawaii, or, best of all, simply "hanging out," laughing and playing and staying up until three in the morning and sleeping until three in the afternoon. This was more fun for me than figuring out the next business plan. Now, for some people the business plan is it, but not for me. And yet sharing with and inspiring large audiences reached through the ministry was the *greatest* experience of love I had ever known (outside of loving my two daughters). I did not immediately see an alternative to the organization that increasingly hemmed me in. So when the man who became my fourth husband came along I thought, Oh great! Finally I can be the joyful, feminine entity I am and have a playmate and friend to dance through life with.

The Selling of Religion

I was becoming weary of big-business religion. It was becoming basically a buying and selling job. And all the while I was telling myself, You're doing it only for Jesus and only for God. But the truth is that I was doing it for myself . . . and that was a hard awakening.

• • •

Religion is the same as business. Like business, it must keep growing and producing more services or products—"saving" more lost souls—in order to succeed. It's a conflict-oriented game with winners and losers. But winning in this game carries a price. The conflict places stress on your body and on your total being.

I longed for peace but also loved the excitement of creation. I was learning that I didn't have to sacrifice one for the other; I could have it all. But that didn't seem likely at the time.

• • •

When I married my fourth husband I discovered that he was a workaholic. Now that was great for him because that was his game, but it was a disappointment to me. I, too, had been a workaholic; now I wanted to be in peace and pleasure. Even so I began thinking, Well, here at least is a person who, because of his self-acknowledged business acumen, can run the organization, so that it keeps getting bigger, keeps enrolling more people. We'll get the television program into more cities and we will have more viewers.

I knew that what I was doing was helpful to people, because as a loving being I asked of people only that they experience the greatness of themselves. And therein lay the crux of the problem. It is a problem faced by all leaders, spiritual or political. They know what they're doing they do for themselves—if they are truly honest—and yet even in that knowingness they see that others are benefiting from it, often enormously. So it becomes almost a seduction. How do you stop something that you know, by the evidence of your own eyes, is so good for so many? That becomes the question.

The Solution and the Dichotomy

It took a long time—from 1981 to 1985—for me to go from "Well, this husband will be the answer, a partner who can both run the ministry while I am the message giver and be my playmate and a friend," to the realization "I am on my own and always have been on my own. My life is more important than my crusade, my life is more important than my cause."

I also came to the realization that the cause itself had become self-aggrandizement at one level, even though satisfying and beneficial for people on other levels. It was a wonderful ministry. And still I knew that freedom would come only when I stopped the enslavement program, stopped the sales pitch, and stopped this massive organization from growing in complexity to unmanageable proportions.

What caused me to see all this? Nothing had changed in the ministry (except that it had become larger), so how did it happen that I began to view it in a different way?

It began, I believe, because I had been more committed all along to *my own* spiritual liberation, my own liberation as a person, than to the form in which that came. I also practice what I teach. So I was hearing myself, recognizing the truth as I spoke it.

During this time (most of 1983 and 1984), I began to go more into myself and more into my relationship with God as I know God to be. I began to experience more and more what it cost me to do this thing, to be in this thing called the ministry.

I looked for someone who could run it and set me free but never found that someone. No one could get a handle on it. My husband couldn't, and even though I hired qualified people and paid them big salaries, they couldn't, either. They just added to the burden.

I'm sure that part of what made it difficult for others to grab the ministry and take it somewhere without me was that I couldn't entirely let go of it. I wouldn't let it go even though I wanted to give it away. It was a classic paradox. The ministry possessed me. What I had created and possessed was possessing *me*. Sound familiar?

Then came the breakthrough.

• • •

March 17, 1985, came and went like any other day in the lives of millions of people all over the world. For me that day will always hold special significance, for that was the day on which I signed my own declaration of independence. My signature took the form of an announcement, one totally unexpected by my congregation that morning—and not all that expected by me.

For months I'd known the end was near. For weeks I'd felt the day of decision at hand. When I awoke that Sunday morning, St. Patrick's Day, I knew the hour had arrived.

I had told no one what was going on within me, although I can't believe it was that much of a surprise to those who knew me well. One thing after another had been pointing toward the enormous changes that were taking place within me, and even the most casual observer must have had some silent suspicion. A series of six major events would have provided dramatic indications to anyone watching closely. These events included:

- The dissolution of my marriage in early 1984

- My connection with and formation of a personal relationship with Reuben in August of that year

- My trip to Israel and the events there in the fall of 1984

- My trip to India and what happened to me there in February 1985

- Television and radio interviews with me in Chicago at the end of February 1985

- My one-week retreat with "Ramtha," a spiritual teacher, in Yucca Valley, California, early in March of 1985

• • •

The end of my fourth marriage was at first devastating to me. I began to reexperience the feelings of low self-worth and failure that had always accompanied the dissolution of previous relationships. But this time I stayed in the Holy Spirit in a state of love with myself, and I was quickly lifted into a greater understanding.

Staying in the Holy Spirit is simply a matter of keeping your heart, your mind, and your thoughts all focused on the same place—on love. To accomplish this requires mental discipline at first, but it gradually begins to come so naturally that one is automatically suffused with thoughts of love. What I did to achieve this state was never to allow my thoughts to drift toward self-recrimination, self-condemnation, self-hatred, or self-denial. Each time I felt myself beginning to drift in one or all of those directions, I consciously stopped whatever I was doing and literally *changed my mind.* I shifted my thoughts instead to the truth: that I am God's perfect creation and everything that occurs happens according to God's perfect plan, that there is no such thing as a mistake and that because I have made what I *consider* to be an error is no reason to harshly judge myself. I affirmed that every action I take is but a stepping-stone to my own highest learning and highest good, that all I have ever wanted for myself and all others is the greatest experience of love. I acknowledged my willingness to create and share the experience of love with all whose lives I touch and reaffirmed my oneness with God in this endeavor. (It is easy to remain in love with myself when I think such thoughts. The truth always sets us free.)

While my marriage was by no means perfect, we both tried very hard to hold it together, all the while hoping to mold it into our own personal ideal. The truth was that the relationship was complete; the wisdom we both needed we had received. The relationship served me well and was another necessary part of my life that I am happy I experienced exactly as I did. You dance together in life until you no longer receive joy and value, and then—contrary to popular belief—it is time for the next adventure.

We ended the relationship—with love—and went our separate ways. Now I had to face my ministry as a woman alone once more. I quickly realized how happy I was to be my own person. I had once again freed myself and in my new-found freedom discovered fun and joy beyond what I had experienced in my marriage. I did not want to jump into another intimate relationship. It was time for me to go deeper into myself and to be responsible at a new level. So I kept on keeping on, as they say, continued to tell the truth to myself and others and moved to the next experience.

A New Gift, a New Joy

Reuben is a totally free, loving being. At nineteen he knew that he did not want to be lost in the American system and left his home to go to India. He wanted to be himself and live from himself. He went to India to seek his spiritual truth.

For six months he was a "spiritual madman," as he describes it. He wandered around the Himalayas. He traveled the streets as a beggar. He did whatever he was called to do by the spiritual masters he encountered along the way. He explored every major religion—Hinduism, Buddhism, Judaism, Christianity.

Then, when he was complete, he left them behind to follow the God of his being.

After five years Reuben returned to the United States. One Sunday morning in San Francisco he saw me on television, and something I said clicked. Hearing an announcement about one of my classes at the end of the program, he showed up at the registration table at the next class session. He enjoyed the class that night and later told me that what he learned was "about the sanest thing I've heard since returning to America."

• • •

My first meeting with Reuben came at a time in my life when I had been exposed to some very significant messages about myself. In my former marriage I had come to believe that I was unfeminine and unlovable, that I was vicious and attacking and unsensual. Luckily, I had a high self-esteem, so I did not accept this as the truth. However, I did begin to close off my sensuality and femininity. I wondered, Will I ever have that feeling again?

When my marriage ended, I decided I was not going to do anything artificial or unnatural to see if I could answer the question. I told myself I was not going to go on dates or play sexual games, that I didn't care if I never went out with another man. I was living for myself and would only make love when my energy moved in that direction as I felt a bonding and a blending beyond the physical body. I would not be a pawn or allow myself to be used, nor would I use anyone else in order to be accepted.

I did none of those things with Reuben. We were together with no hidden agendas, with no expectations. And all at once the energy began to flow and I was alive again and I was beautiful again. And it happened in just the blink of an eye, because I wasn't planning it and I wasn't looking for it. I was simply loving myself.

Reuben and I have been in each other's presence ever since.

Our relationship is an adventure that is created moment to moment. Every day we reaffirm the truth of love—that is to desire for another all that that person chooses for him- or herself while living true to oneself.

• • •

Why have I chosen to tell you about Reuben? Why have I embarked on the revelation of details of my personal life more intimate and personal than any details I have ever revealed before? Because I promised you at the outset that this would be more than the simple story of how a ministry was born, grew, and came to its natural conclusion. I said it would be the sharing of a personal journey, from imprisonment to liberation, and my experience with Reuben has been as much a part of that liberation as any single experience of my life.

3. Israel and Other Realities

*There are some who say that because
man was created in the image of God,
one who honors all human beings is in effect
honoring the Lord,
whom we are obliged to honor*

The Living Talmud
Chapter IV

I left my world of organization behind in October 1984 and traveled with Reuben to Israel. There we were together in a wonderful partnership of the soul. We had an agreement that there were to be no attachments, no expectations, no obligations or system to our being together. It was what it was and would be that until it changed. This was a new way for me to experience a relationship. It was at once bonding and freeing, pulling in and letting out, not so very different from the physical act of love itself. And that is exactly what we were doing in every minute of the relationship. We were, quite literally, making love.

I felt I could be me, truly me, for the first time within the confines of a twosome as we had created it, and precisely because as we had created it there were no confines.

The freedom I began to experience led to the experience of freedom in the entirety of my existence. The day I was truly set free was Yom Kippur. On the beach. At Caesarea. It was a day I will never forget.

There, looming out of the ocean in front of us, were Roman columns from the time of Caesar and, nearby, a Roman aqueduct built at the time of Jesus. It was where Herod had lived and where John the Baptist is said to have been beheaded. There also were relics from the Crusades, one of humanity's many misguided adventures wherein mankind killed and pillaged and plundered . . . in the name of God.

We sat there among the ruins, where one can just walk around and pick up pieces of pottery and stonework left from that incredible time in human history.

Because it was Yom Kippur, no one else was on the beach. And if we had driven, zealots might well have stoned us . . . in the name of God . . . on the Day of Atonement. And I began to see in that moment that our entire planet was stuck in a place of pulling and tearing and religious misunderstanding, and nowhere is this more clearly evident than in Israel.

Here lie the foundations of the Jewish/Christian ethic. Here also is a holy place of the Moslems. And here, too, the heretics and the nonbelievers will be found, as well as those who still seek, not knowing which way to turn or who was or is right. Here, perhaps more than in any other single place, the fact that *no one* was or is right becomes immediately apparent.

We realized then, Reuben and I, that we had come to this time and this place—one a Jew, the other a Christian—in order for us both to transcend our enslavement to belief systems that would otherwise bind us in resentment, anger, and self-righteousness forever, and to escape from the madness of murder in the name of God.

We played and we swam, and I laughed and I danced on the beach.

It was a day of liberation in a place of bondage to tradition. And if this wasn't the way God wanted it, if this joy and this peace and this togetherness, Jew with Christian, male with female, soul with soul, was against the highest wish of God, then the highest wish of God was lower than the highest wish of Man. That thought showed itself at once to be preposterous and therefore led me to the truth, which only made Reuben and me laugh loud and long and louder still, until the waves crashed in around us and the sounds of the sea drowned us out. We became still and at peace and at one on this day of at-one-ment.

I left this world behind on that day. I was a playful child. I was myself. For the first time, I experienced my true self.

Once you open that door, once you have that feeling, you can never turn back, you can never be quite the same again.

And I am not.

The Loss of Peace

Then it was time to come home. Neither of us wanted to leave Israel, but neither of us could give ourselves permission to stay. On the plane returning home I began to get irritable. I hated having to return, hated having to go to the ministry offices, hated having to face the endless decisions and devise the endless strategies for being More and Bigger and Better. I loved the Sunday talks—I always loved the talks. And I loved the writing. But I hated the rest.

When I got back, the organization was madness, with every-one running on fear and everyone enslaved to my plans, as I was enslaved to theirs—keeping a job . . . building an empire . . .

We had a debt. As always, we were behind in money. Many organizations operate that way—always behind—so I didn't feel guilt about this so much as pressure. There was a constant demand to bring in more money.

I was back home only two days and already I was asking myself, "What happened? What happened to the peace and the joy and the comfort of the soul? What happened?" I remembered that in Israel I had been happy. I could be with ordinary people; I could sit in a store in the walled city of Jerusalem with an Arab shopkeeper and have a cup of Turkish coffee and chat. I was free. It didn't matter what I had. It didn't matter what I didn't have.

I began to see that I would have to take back my organization and make it what I wanted it to be. So I took the first step and rounded up some key players to help me. This was late in the fall of 1984, just before Thanksgiving. I told those I had gathered around me that I wanted to bring the ministry into a state of financial integrity, that I wanted to know what was going on, and that I had decided to be "here, right here in the office" (where I rarely came), in order to stay on top of things.

I thought that if I could create an organization that worked effectively, even if I had to do it primarily by myself, it could just run without me once this groundwork was done. Then I could travel. I could lecture on occasion. I could play and be who I am. I could be free.

Some of the key people with whom I had worked, good friends, saw in my decision the end of the ministry. In truth, that is what it was. It was the end of a dream, and when any dream ends there are many reactions. Some of the ministry staff felt happy, released. Others were angry, confused. Some felt they had to leave.

In the midst of this, I was making attempts to hold it together. I took five of my key people—those who would be on the new team—to Hawaii, where we worked for a week with a business consultant who helped us define what we all wanted to do.

We created a plan, an organizational setup, that promised in time—in five or six months—to bring everything under control and into order. We came back from that week all ready to go. Everything was laid out before me, including our entire financial situation. And then I found out that all the time *I had not known what was going on*—where we were financially, where we were organizationally, where we were, period. I also understood that I hadn't wanted to know. Nobody could have kept anything from me without my wanting them to.

I realized then that there was a part of me—the fear that I had that everything would fall apart (which is sometimes the drive to keep it going)—that nobody wanted to see. People would not tell me things they thought would upset me. And that was because of my reaction. If they tried to give me their opinion or their point of view, I closed them off. So because they wanted to be with me, they stopped sharing. People around me had begun to feel as if they were not there, that it didn't matter if I took their advice or not. That wasn't the real issue. The real issue was that everyone had their truth, but I was so afraid that their truth would be an invalidation of me, that it meant I was wrong or a failure, that I allowed no room for it.

Also, I didn't like anger; I didn't like people's upsets. I felt those were judgments of me, and I already had such harsh judgments of myself that I couldn't handle theirs. I'm still not totally healed of that, but it's getting better now, and soon I will be in a place where I love myself enough to allow others to say whatever they wish, acknowledging their truth and letting it be.

Everything I have described created a wall of "Don't tell Terry." That actually became a password within the ministry: "Don't tell Terry. Don't let her know that."

What's ironic about this is that on the other hand I loved strong people who would say, "Hey, Terry, don't give me your bull. I'm going to tell you what I think." I *loved* that. I *longed* for people who wouldn't be afraid of me, who would tell me the truth.

Another Level of the Dream

In any event, after returning from Hawaii I learned what the true status of the ministry was: We were sixty to ninety days behind in paying our bills and thus deeply in debt. I realized we would have to make major cuts in our financial outflow, which we did. Then we devised a plan to get us current within three to four months.

The plan worked, but there was one thing wrong with it. Even as the back debts were being taken care of and the organization was being reduced in size and put back in order, I noticed that I wasn't feeling any better. I wasn't happy.

It was then that I woke up to yet another level of the dream that I called my life and began consciously to experience the enslavement I spoke of earlier. I also began to fear that I might be assassinated. All people who are perceived as saviors are. John Kennedy, Bobby Kennedy, Martin Luther King, Jr., Gandhi. Yet this should be a time when you are not killed for your beliefs, for this is a new age.

I came to a sudden awareness that in many previous lifetimes I had been killed and tortured for my beliefs, just as in many lifetimes I had killed and tortured others for theirs. I also knew that this time around I didn't want just another life. I wanted this to be my last time on this planet. This is a beautiful planet, and I choose to bring love to it.

I also realized that my life was more important than dying, and I could see what I was doing to myself. The bigger I became as a religious leader, the more fanatics came out of the woodwork. I remembered Oral Roberts telling me that he has to live with walls and a guard around his house. That can make you feel that you have a mission, I suppose, and yet no one has really come to save the world. We all have come to save ourselves.

This is no longer a time of one Christ. This is a time of all being Christ, because the Christ is you—when you know who you are and bring that into your experience.

There were threats on my life, and suddenly I was facing other hostilities I never had faced before. Lawsuits in which I was accused of things that never happened, that never could have happened (but I had to face the accusations anyway, just because I was well known). The press was attacking me. On television programs, it was evident that people were not as interested in my message as they were in my private life and in what I was doing with *the money*.

All of people's fears having to do with God and their own sovereignty and power were pushed at me. The more alive I was, the happier I was, the more abundant I was, the more I began living for myself, the more flak I received because I was in religion. I could see that I was setting myself up to be a martyr. I was setting myself up as a celebrity, as someone from whom newscasters and the press could make a living.

I realized clearly, in those moments before I went all the way and really *did* create myself as a full-fledged celebrity, that we truly create one another. The celebrities create the columnists and the columnists create the celebrities. And it is the same way in the world at large. The good guys create the bad guys and the bad guys create the good guys so they all can be who they are. But when you have found yourself, you don't need the challenge of proving yourself to the world anymore.

The Adventure in India

In February of 1985 I went to India, once again traveling with Reuben. I had no way of knowing that this would be the fourth of six major events leading up to a shift in my entire way of life. I had the desire when I left to help bring the United States and India together. I saw the United States as representing the male principle, or the male energy, and India as representing the female.

The concept I had was that I would interview some of the Indian leaders and myself try to "become India," become the experience that we call poverty, become the experience that we call passive. In so doing, I would balance my Self, because I am an American, a Western person who has lived in a Western society and has Western values. So I went there totally open to having the experience of the blending of myself.

It was my intention to show India on American television not as a place of poverty or helplessness, but as a place populated with enlightened, loving, caring beings who reflect the feminine principle. I hoped that my trip and the film I would shoot for exposure on my nationwide television program would somehow provide an opportunity for balancing out the energies of American hostility and Indian resentment, the American male assertiveness and the Indian female receptivity.

I had a vision that if India and America came together and joined as one, it would lift the entire planet.

Five minutes after my plane landed in Nepal I lost touch with all of my highest intentions. I took one look around and thought, Dear God, what have I done to myself? Where am I going to go to the toilet? Can I eat the food? Will I get sick? (Everyone had told me I was sure to get sick.) Here I was hanging out in this unimagined poverty when I had just left La Jolla and my beautiful home with an ocean view. The most charitable way to describe my initial reaction is that it wasn't what I was used to.

After a few minutes of entertaining these thoughts, I got off it, as my friend Werner Erhard would say. I said to myself, "Great, so be *here*. You are the master, so you won't be sick unless you choose to be." (I never did get sick.)

I decided to give up my judgments completely. Soon I could be found spending time in the temples with the Hindus and the Buddhists and the beggars. I began to be in relationship with these people. I found them to be myself—and also to be much happier than most people I have known. They look you in the eye and they're *with* you, and they're magnificent.

It was a great adventure. I went to a street market, and I can't tell you how much more enlivening this was than going to a supermarket at home. Buying and selling there is a ritual rather than a cold, impersonal exchange. These people were selling personal goods and services, and every merchant had his reputation and his family's name on the line. I could feel the electricity in the air. There was *life* in that street market. There was *livingness*.

You will find more living in the so-called Third World countries than you ever will in the so-called First World countries, because in the First World countries we protect ourselves from our own feelings and needs and desires and hopes and, in a horrifying sense, from our very lives. We have become incarcerated in emotional and physical encasements of our own making. These encasements keep us antiseptic, all right, but they also keep us separate. There is no *encounter*. (You don't know what encounter is until you go to a street market in Nepal!)

I moved on to India . . . and loved it. I was happy, and that was beginning to reign supreme for me. Wherever I was, I intended to be happy.

Saying Hello to Sai Baba

One of the highlights of this trip was a journey to see Sai Baba, who in India is considered a guru and a genuine holy man. People sit outside of his house and worship. I observed this carefully and suddenly saw how I could do that, too— literally get people to worship me. It might take a slightly different form, yet it would be worship nonetheless. And in that moment I knew that you can tell people you are God and they are not, you can tell people you are the Lord of Lords, you can tell people you are an avatar, you can tell people you are anything and get them to believe it. They will sit outside your house waiting for you to pass by because they want to be in your energy rather than be in their own.

I saw people who had been living there in Sai Baba's space for years, giving their power to this man they saw as the God of Gods.

I decided to get caught up in it, too. I turned to Reuben and said, "I'll play the game," because I thought, Well, it's my ego that won't let me humble myself, so I'll humble myself. I will do whatever it takes.

I even thought, Well, maybe he's It. And if he's It, why

should I stand in the way of what's going to bring me ultimate liberation? I will surrender to him. And all the people there believe he *is* It. They disapprove of you if you dare to wear flowers around your neck. Only Baba can wear flowers, because he's the Divine One. Whatever happens to anyone in the community, you hear the same thing from everyone else in the community: "Baba did it."

It was then that I began to realize that in all religions, whoever is the leader is It, and for you *not* to think they're It is blasphemy. I put flowers around my neck, and the people there had a fit because *I* wasn't the Holy of Holies, *I* wasn't the Divine One, *I* wasn't the Lord of Lords. I was but this meager mortal thinking, Hey, I'm as good as this guy. Blasphemy!

If in this world you proclaim yourself to be, you will find there is that element that says you're not. But there is also the element that knows you are because it is. That is the element, those are the people I like to play with! I can be as powerful as I am because they are powerful in themselves, not threatened but inspired by being with me, as I am with them. We are equals, becoming greater in each other's presence.

When we got in to see Sai Baba I noticed how much power I gave to him. Everybody gave him power. And then when I got to *be* with him I noticed how much love came through, how much peace. He was *himself*. He was a *player*. He was *fun*. He was a magician. He and I connected a lot. We held hands and he said, "I am always with you, and you are with me." He told everyone, "You are God and I am God," and in that I felt the joining of our beings. It was an awesome experience of love. Everyone wept. All of us felt this incredible wave of love and feeling. It was wonderful. This wasn't the first time. I had felt it before. But the feeling was wonderful, and I was so free and so happy . . .

• • •

I returned from India a much different person from what I was when I left. There were people waiting for me to announce that I was a Sai Baba devotee, which I'm not. I love him dearly, but I am not a devotee of any guru. I am a devotee of myself. And I am a devotee of you because *you are me* and *I am you*.

When I returned from India I had truly awakened to the fact that every beggar was equal to me, every king and queen was equal to me, every great spiritual master was the same as I, and what makes the difference between masters is that one master knows he is a master and the other doesn't. When you know it, you step into the arrogant and the humble at the same time. You become both.

Now, you don't have to go and stand on the street corner and tell everyone that you are God or great. You simply must know it within yourself. Just knowing it within yourself feeds the soul of humanity, lifting all mankind into the Light.

My First Public Sharing of Changes Within

If my time on the beach in Israel at Yom Kippur had been my day of personal freedom, my time in India marked the beginning of my professional liberation. Those who listened closely to my talk on February 17 could not miss what I was communicating that Sunday. I listened to the tape of that sermon recently, and here are some excerpts:

> It was an incredible, incredible experience. Every day was Raiders of the Lost Ark. A real adventure. I went to Nepal and learned many things. One thing that was fascinating is that begging there is a profession. It's a job. And if you were to give a beggar something beautiful to wear, he or she would have to put it away because how can one beg in a new outfit?
>
> Well . . . just look at how attached you are to your rap and your act . . . and me to mine. Someone tells you to change it and you say, "Yeah? Well, what am I gonna do?"
>
> There was this one man who was a Sheba Babba, and he was smoking his hash and dressed up in his orange robe . . . and he couldn't see very well, so he had this note, which he handed us. It said that he wanted money to get an eye operation. So I said to

him, "Well, we'll heal you." So I did this incredible healing . . . and he couldn't see any better when it was over than before I'd begun. I learned something incredible from that. How could you have an instant healing if then you were faced with how you were going to raise money? I mean, it looked like an old note. He'd been asking for money for that operation forever. And of course he'll probably never have enough because he'll only get enough to make ends meet . . .

What was fascinating was that I had the healing experience because healing is instant, and anyone who wants an instant healing gets it. Whoever wants to experience it instantly does. But you have to want it. You have to be willing to give up whatever payoff you're getting out of being sick.

And what I realized in the whole trip . . . well, actually I realized a lot . . . but what was clear to me is that it's always a choice. A lot of people don't want to say that we have a choice. But there is no life-style better or worse than another. There is no life more right or more wrong. All beings have the right to choose their existence. I think the problem is that we don't know we have the choice. That's when poverty is a problem—when you don't know you have a choice. But when you know you have a choice, you are never poor.

In India, at Sai Baba's ashram, we slept on cement floors. And you take cold baths with a bucket. You ladle out the water and throw it all over yourself in the morning. It's very primitive living compared to what we do, but . . . my energy never changed. I was always happy.

And you know what was so great? To see a country full of basically happy people.

There weren't any delinquents. Their kids were working. They construct the buildings by hand, so everyone has a job—something to do.

And they have wild drivers. Just wild. The road to the Taj Mahal was amazing. Our driver was a master. He could tell how long someone had been driving. His timing . . . he was perfectly in the moment. There, if your attention lapses for one second, it's all over.

They're playing the consciousness game as if their lives depend on it, and they're out in the fast lane. To pass cars, they go into the oncoming traffic. Is that fun? You just have no idea!

And there are oxen and buffalo pulling these big wagons, plus buses and trucks and tractors and people walking and riding bicycles . . . all on the same side of the road.

. . . and they only use the gas pedal and horn . . .

And the wrecks are the most incredible you have ever seen, because it's all or nothing. Talk about living on the edge!

Well . . . today's talk is called "The Only Path to Heaven." What I've noticed is that everyone always thinks they have the only way . . . and that's usually their way. What I can share with you is my experience, but ultimately you always have to make your own decisions. No one can decide for you, no one can take the responsibility for your life, no one has your answers.

I am not your guru. I am not even your teacher. You teach yourself. I can't teach you anything you don't already know. And when you are ready to awaken to that, you will create me or someone else to say whatever needs to be said or to be whatever needs to be in order for you to recognize what is already there.

You are God. I am God. Together we are God. And together, through our own conscious awakening and choice, we create the kingdom of God.

Later in the same talk I told the congregation:

This is the age, this is the time of awakening. This is the time of the Light; this is the time of the Christ.

Now, when I speak about the Christ, do not confuse it with Christianity, okay? You can confuse the Christ with Christianity, just as you can confuse any master with the message. You then take on the personality of the one delivering the message or of the cult organization that grew up around that individual. Don't do that."

I asked them to look at all religions of the world and see how many teach fear, teach hate, teach vengeance, teach anger. Are they not teaching murder and war in the name of God?

Finally, in a very quiet voice, I told them:

In my spiritual journey I have tested myself or been tested. And I have often, often, often not trusted myself.

You see, you shouldn't even believe me. To believe me is to give me more power than you have, and when you want your power

*back, you will want to kill me so that you can be who you are . . .
you will want to find something wrong with me so that you can be
okay. That's because you do not see yourself in me. Separation
always leads to attack.*

*But we can, if we choose, join together in a common purpose, in
the Truth and the Light. And in that joining together, we will lift
all beings into the Light. We have an opportunity in this world—
and now is the time—to be the Light.*

4. Chicago: The Turning Point

When I came back from India, the whole system of living up to other people's expectations, of fitting in socially, suddenly seemed ridiculous to me.

I was experiencing a great spiritual awakening. This spiritual awakening that had drawn me to India awakened fear at the same time. My ego was afraid of losing its last remnants of control. I somehow knew that India would be the final step in a process that had been going on for several years, a process of divesting myself of ego.

That process reached a peak at the end of February 1985, when I traveled to Chicago for a series of media appearances that had been scheduled weeks in advance. I felt I had to make those appearances in order to keep my word to the journalists who had waited for me to get back to the States. The Chicago trip was a major turning point in my life, although I had no idea it was going to be that when I stepped on that plane at San Diego's Lindbergh Field.

So often we miss major turning points in our lives because we are not looking for them in our day-to-day routine. We think that they are going to show up in the special events and moments of our lives, but that isn't how it happens. Every encounter, every relationship, every moment in your day-to-day experience becomes an awesome experience when you are totally conscious. Life then is not about waiting until you meet the right person or have the big job. It is about observing yourself in your moment-to-moment activities.

The Chicago experience turned out to be a series of mundane, moment-to-moment activities out of which sprang a pivotal event in my lifelong journey to today. Interviews by print and broadcast journalists all may seem very exciting—and, in fact, they are . . . until you do your 267th. Then they sink slowly to the level of the humdrum and the mundane. If one is not careful, they can even turn into events to be avoided. Fascinating. That which one wanted so badly at one point in life suddenly becomes something to be avoided.

On my schedule for this late February media swing through the Windy City was a television interview program before a live audience. I was appearing with a gentleman evangelist. I thought I'd been asked on the program to discuss my ideas about God and religion and man's higher purpose—things like that. But the line of questioning once again was: Are you fleecing the public by receiving donations? What do you do with the money? How much do you receive in contributions in the average week and month?

Everything was money-related, and I saw once again how much stress people attach to money simply because they don't know that they are creators. They don't know that they are unlimited. They don't even know that money is just a means of exchange. They are angry about money. They hate it, they love it, they can't do without it, they don't know what to do with it, and if you've got it—and especially if people have *given* it to you—they are totally strung out.

I knew what was going on, of course. Sitting there under the hot studio lights with the audience four feet in front of me and the cameras staring me in the face, I knew exactly what was going on. Very soon after the program began, my host began to attack both my colleague and myself. She had to begin this way in order to assure a good program. I know how that works. I even know why it works. I know that it *has* to work that way or these people won't be on the air very long. Still, I played right into it.

Somewhere in the middle of the program I heard a voice screaming. For an instant I thought someone had gone mad. Then I realized the voice was inside my head. It said, "Hey, you don't have to *do* this! In your own peace you just play and laugh and sing and dance. What are you doing here? Why are you taking this message to people who don't want it? Is *this* what you want? Is this what you're after?"

Then, in the middle of a barbed question, an argument started. But this, too, was inside my head. I felt as if I were being attacked from *within* as well as from without. The interviewer was jumping all over me with negativity, and suddenly this debate was raging inside of me, a second voice saying, "Listen, if you *don't* get this message out there, the ministry won't grow and you won't be saving souls and making the world a better place. You want the whole thing to fall apart? You want to be a failure? Of *course* she's interrogating you. You asked for it, didn't you? Stop being a baby and answer the questions."

I shook the voices away in what must have looked on camera like an annoyed, defiant "no" gesture and focused hard on the words coming at me from the outside. I answered the question I was asked, and I tried hard to smile. I remember thinking, How can I say this now without getting everybody all upset? I managed to do it. I even got a few laughs. Then my heart sank. I realized with a sickening inner thud what I'd just done—and what I'd been doing since I walked into that studio.

First, I'd allowed myself to lose my peace out of some inner need to justify my existence and my methods. Then I saw

myself selling out my integrity. I'm *people-pleasing*, I told
myself. I'm sitting here pushing the ministry like some *pro-
moter*.

The Radio Announcer Who "Saved" My Life

All at once I felt tired. Very, very tired. The program was
over and someone was guiding my body to a side door and into
a car, and within minutes, after careening in and out of Chicago
traffic, I found myself deposited in the lobby of a radio station.
Everyone was being very solicitous and telling me how glad
they were that I could make this interview. They gave the
name of the man who was going to interview me. Was it Jim or
was it Todd? I couldn't seem to hold the name in my head.
Well, it was *somebody*, anyway, and he had a talk show on
Chicago radio so he must be at least a little important because,
after all, this wasn't Podunk, Iowa, and . . .

Believe me, this is how your mind works, when you're doing
twelve hours of these shows in one day. They led me into the
radio announcer's booth while one of the commercials was
running. Actually, somebody grabbed me by the arm and
practically threw me in there. "Okay, c'mon!" they said,
"we've got a commercial break!" In I went. A man behind a
microphone looked up at me, headphones on his ears, a ciga-
rette dangling from his mouth. "You're Cole-Whittaker,
right?" he asked. I felt as if I were in jail.

"Yes," I mumbled and sat down just before somebody
seemed about to shove me into a chair. They were adjusting a
second microphone to get it closer to me. It came at me from
overhead. Someone else gave me a headset. "You know how to
wear these?" they asked. (How can you not know how to wear
a headset? You put 'em on your *ears*, for heaven's sake!)

I felt myself losing my cool. I took a deep breath. The
announcer introduced himself and tried to put me at ease.
"Okay, there's nothing going on here," he soothed, "we're just

going to chat back and forth and I'm going to ask you some questions, all right?"

I nodded without a sound, because just as I was going to say something he put his finger to his lips with a terse whisper. "Coming out," he rasped. I figured they must have been coming out of the commercial. I figured right.

It was then that I realized I wasn't in jail at all. I was in this man's kingdom. This was his domain, and I was his captive. Within those walls and in that tiny space I was totally at his mercy. He was a god there, just as we all are within our kingdoms. And he had his constituency, he had his followers, he had his life-style. And I began to understand just exactly what I'd been doing again. I'd been traipsing all over the world, walking into other people's domains, onto their territories, and many times my mere presence overwhelmed their existence!

He began.

"Good morning, Chicago, we're here again going into another hour and our guest now is a lady from California . . . the land of milk and honey known as Southern California . . . whom you may have heard of. She's a television evangelist [he said the word *evangelist* the way you'd say *snake*] . . . a television *evangelist*, name of Terry Cole-Whittaker. Terry, welcome to the program. Can I call you Terry or do I call you 'Reverend'?"

I was embarrassed for him at the question. I don't even know what I said. And then he began—right where the lady interviewer left off. Somewhere in the middle I managed to get a few words in about the principles I teach and the purpose of life on earth as I understand it. Then, abruptly, he cut into one of the few times I'd strung more than three sentences together.

"I don't believe a word you're saying," he bellowed. "What you're saying is a bunch of rot. You're just fleecing the public. Yes, *fleecing* them, madam, that's what I said. Now, I'm not saying what you're telling us doesn't work for you, but it doesn't work for anybody else. Don't you ever cry? Don't you see how bad off the world is? You come in here with your Pepsodent smile and your Gucci handbag and your California tan and you're trying to tell Chicagoans about getting through *life*?"

I could see why some people loved this man.

"Tell me something, ma'am, if it isn't too much," he went on. "What are you *doing* this for?"

I froze. The question absolutely froze me. I thought, Yes, Terry, *what are you doing this for*? Then I asked myself a follow-up question. Why should I disturb my peace, joy, bliss, and happiness to save the world, to make the ministry bigger, to generate more income and get more people to watch a television program sending a message many of them didn't even want?

Again, as in the television studio just moments before, I had the impression that I was cramming something down people's throats and, conversely, actually feeling *called to* as a world savior. I even felt guilty because *I* was happy and peaceful and abundant and content. I felt—for the first time in many years—that if I had all this and wasn't giving it to others, I should be ashamed, because it wasn't *right* for me to have all this freedom when the world was living in pain.

The truth is, I was living the principles I was teaching. I was becoming a master, just as anybody can. But I realized and saw in that moment that it was not my responsibility to do it for somebody else. I couldn't if I wanted to. Plus (and this was a *big* "plus"), *others are right to live as they choose!* There is no one, single right way and no one, single truth. Everybody's truth is right for them. And I came to an incredible knowingness in that moment that this man, in his kingdom, in his radio booth, was living his truth. Of course he couldn't see my truth! And I couldn't see his. His kingdom was as it should be because he was getting the wisdom from what he was doing that he needed for his soul completion. And I was doing what I needed for *my* soul-completion. We were two equal gods, entities, sons of God—call it what you will—on our own path to our own salvation, the salvation you achieve when you wake up and accept who you are and begin to live.

I don't remember exactly what I said in answer to my wonderful radio announcer's question. I remember stumbling over the words I was saying because I felt I had to justify myself, and so I talked in sort of a weak voice. I think I said something like, "Well, because it helps people."

"How do you know it helps anybody?" he demanded.

I looked at him almost sheepishly. "Well . . . from the letters they write and the things they say to me." And I began to think, Yeah, how *do* I know?

And that's how it came to pass that I had a direct experience of this radio announcer as *me*, talking to myself, and saying the things that I hadn't had the courage to say. He blessed me.

I walked out of the radio station feeling a lot of confusion, a lot of upset. What if what I did never made any difference? But the truth is, it made a difference to *me*. *I* was better off. My ministry was better off. And the people in it were, too. There were people in this ministry who got their lives back because they gave of themselves. Contribution worked. Service worked. Playing 100 percent worked. It all worked for them.

Yet I knew in that moment that if somebody doesn't want to go down my path, whatever they're doing works for them. I don't have anybody's truth.

I returned from Chicago knowing that it was time for me to go somewhere, to be alone, to think, to ponder. I had major life decisions to make. I knew I couldn't make them if I stayed in the same environment, going to work every day. I felt a change coming on, and I knew I couldn't work through what that was going to be while daily standing alongside people who had an investment in my staying the same. I could get all the advice I wanted from them, but it would always be their truth. I knew I had to go somewhere where I would hear a *cosmic* truth that was hard hitting, impersonal, void of ego. It was time for me to become me.

It was time for me to become . . . me.

5. My Ministry Is Over

*You cannot guide whom you please: it is Allah
who guides whom He will. He knows best those
who yield to guidance.*

The Koran
28:56

I can remember in March of 1985 making an active decision
to be a sovereign whole person and no longer a product of
the world. Products of the world are those who believe themselves to be nothing more than what the world has made of
them, the result of accidents of birth, environment, upbring-
ing, social class, financial standing, education, background, and
experience. Most people view themselves as products of the
world, and this is understandable because most of us know no
other reality. There is another reality, but to begin living from
it you must let go of this world, as well as your past.

When you are in your mind, or in your head, about things,
the place you are coming from is usually very logical, very
methodical, very sensible, and very experience- or proof-
based. Your understanding is limited to what you have experienced directly or what someone else has experienced directly
and can communicate to you.

To begin living as a sovereign being you must move out of
the space of your mind and refuse to be limited by what it tells

you. You move out of social consciousness and world beliefs and no longer direct your life as an extension of what *others* think. You become your own hero, your own ideal, and you live from your own truth.

You must also be willing to let go of this world and not limit yourself by thinking that you are nothing more than the end result of the worldly life you have lived, the worldly goods you have been given, the worldly possessions you have earned, and the worldly accolades you have been seeking.

When you are willing to begin living as if you are no longer a product of the world, then in fact you *are* no longer a product of the world *and the world no longer owns you.* When the world no longer owns you, you are its master, its ruler. You find that there is nothing in the world without which you cannot exist. You are happy at all times, in all places and circumstances. You are truly in this world but not of it. You are truly the creator of your experience and therefore the master of your world. You are complete in and of yourself. You are a sovereign and whole person.

The Last Major Event

Earlier, I said that six major events played a role in my choice to become sovereign and whole and no longer a product of this world. So far I've talked about five of them. The sixth was by far the most unusual and the most important—most important because this was the event that pushed me over the edge. I am speaking of my first meeting with a 35,000-year-old entity named Ramtha.

You may think me an eccentric even to tell you about any of this (after all, I did have *some* credibility up until now), but that couldn't matter less. I am committed to telling you exactly what happened to me in those last months of my four-year struggle to reach a decision about myself and the ministry, and that's exactly what I am doing.

This whole experience started for me in late 1984, when

someone gave me a set of cassette tapes made by a woman known as J. Z. Knight, who claims to be a channel for an entity called Ramtha. Now, I obviously am not in a position to judge scientifically whether this woman is a channel, nor do I care to. I need no proof. Moreover, the question of veracity never even occurred to me. Why? Because the cassette tapes I heard and the message I received rang true for me. It is what I wanted and what I needed to hear. It is also what I teach. The message made my heart jump for joy, and it created exactly what I knew I needed when I came back from Chicago: a place where I could go to create space for myself that would allow me to make the decisions I knew I must make.

Thus it was that I went to Yucca Valley, California, a few miles north of Palm Springs, for a week-long retreat with J. Z. Knight and Ramtha, who is, incidentally, an entity from whom Shirley Maclaine has learned. (I met Shirley at the retreat and really enjoyed our sisterhood. What a courageous, wonderful, and beautiful being she is!)

The focus of the retreat that week was enslavement. It was about how we enslave others to our truth and our way—and become a prisoner ourselves in the process. The message was that your possessions will destroy you. I felt possessed by my own creation, the ministry. It was time to let go and save my life.

Ramtha, who is described as an "ascended master," taught this lesson over and over again throughout the seven days. He is not the only master to have done so. Jesus also taught over and over again to give up the possessions of this world. I have taught it, too. This time as I heard my words coming from another, I listened.

It was either incredibly appropriate or incredibly uncanny that Ramtha's message was exactly the theme of my own life's experience at this point. I realized after only a few moments that it was meant for me to be at this retreat with Shirley and other seekers.

My frame of mind on the way to Yucca Valley was one of

sadness, fear, self-condemnation, and excitement—sadness, because I knew that what the radio talk show host in Chicago had taught me was true; fear, because I didn't know what else I would do if I ever really just quit everything and gave up the ministry; self-condemnation, because of the financial situation the ministry had gotten into (our debt was over three-quarters of a million dollars, and I had to accept that I was responsible for it all); excitement, because I knew I was on the threshold of a whole new adventure.

The head of an organization can only point to inept management or bad advice from spouses or top level players for so long. Then, no matter what the actions of these others might have been, it is time to give up blame, give up resentment, give up anger, and accept complete responsibility for the results around you. I did give up these feelings toward others, but then I directed them toward myself. I had always made judgments about people who didn't know how to handle their money, who were forever in debt, who could not be counted on financially. Now here I was in the same place! And I judged myself. First I judged myself for being in that place. Then I judged myself for ever having judged others for being in that place.

I felt I had done something bad or wrong, when what I really had given with my ministry was a blessing to people, and I had done it out of the highest level of my knowingness at the time. Still, it had the net effect of making me afraid to create anything else. If I were so ignorant that I could have created this situation, then I must be dangerous. I thought, I cause bad things.

I wanted what most people want in times of stress and self-anger and self-pity: I wanted to invalidate myself, rather than to love myself for all the lives that had been blessed and all the joy, happiness, and love people had been made to feel through the ministry.

These were my thoughts as I set out for Yucca Valley. We never know what's going to come out at the other end when we start something. If we knew what was going to happen we probably never would get involved. We would just sit around someplace, never playing in the game of life. But in our ignorance we move into our experiences, *and from our experiences we become enlightened.* The irony of this is that once we become enlightened through our experiences, we learn we are *more* than our experiences.

The Negative Events in Life
Actually Can Free Us

I became enlightened in so many ways. In a very real sense, it was the ministry's debt that freed me, just as that talk show host freed me—and just as *everything that we call negative really is a gift.*

Consider the possibility that the things we don't want to hear really are things we are saying to ourselves. I mean this in the sense that your Higher Self—or God, if you wish—causes you to hear only that which you *need* to hear, that which your Highest Self is actually telling you so that you will take the next step on your evolutionary path. To put this another way, suppose you never heard anything by accident? Suppose there was a *reason* behind everything everyone is saying to you. Suppose there was only one mind, the Universal Mind, and it was doing nothing all day long but speaking to itself? Would this affect to any degree the way in which you hear and receive criticism?

That talk show host in Chicago was really "me" talking to me! As I journeyed to Yucca Valley, I suddenly knew that we can indeed open ourselves to greater happiness, greater love, and less possession by the things we believe we need to possess. We need only open ourselves to the understanding that the whole universe is working in this way to help us attain our own perfection.

• • •

One evening during the retreat I went out into the desert and there spent the hours of the night alone. It was a new experience for me, and it led to an interesting conclusion. Now, you have to understand that I had never been outside in the wilderness all night by myself before—be it the woods or the desert or anywhere else—and for a very good reason. I was afraid. So you can imagine my feeling when it was announced that the workshop directive one particular night was, "Go out into the desert until you find yourself, and when you find yourself, come in."

Just thinking about it made me nervous, even though the sun was still looming cheerfully overhead. "What's the matter with you?" my Critical Parent inner voice asked without mercy. "This is what you wanted, isn't it? Time to be alone? Time for introspection? Time to own your Self?" My Fearful Child, meanwhile, began screaming, "But *wait* a minute! I don't have to go out *there*, do I? I mean, in the desert? At night? Alone? There could be snakes out there! Or wild animals! Or . . . or . . . *men*! They could creep up in the middle of the night and *get* me! Is all this really necessary?"

The campsite area wasn't really that far from the main lodge where the retreat was taking place, and I felt silly thinking such things. Still . . . it was far enough.

A lot of fears come up for a lot of people in the dark, particularly if the darkness is combined with the unknown, and especially if it is the first time. As a child, I was always afraid of the dark—terrified. I was afraid of other people and thought they might have some power over me, that someone could hurt me, could take away my life, my right to exist and to be. All of our fears of being attacked in some way come up for us at times like this.

There is a belief that in reality we all are totally frightened, totally petrified beings roaming this planet and that our only security, what little we may experience, comes from the familiarity of our surroundings.

In any event, here I was in the desert, wondering what I

would do to keep intruding animals away. And then I remembered something significant that an old man at the lodge had
told me just before I left.

"All you have to do to keep animals away is what the
animals do to keep each other away," he sagely advised.

"And what is that?" I asked in my complete naïveté.

"May I be a little . . . indelicate?" he asked. I couldn't
imagine what he was going to say, but whatever it was, I was
sure I'd heard worse.

"I'm going out there to sleep among the snakes and the
critters and I'm worried about some words you might say?" I
laughed. He understood himself to have permission to proceed.

"They urinate."

"They what?"

"They urinate. In a big circle around their area. They stake
their claim in this way, and the scent makes it very clear to the
other animals who owns the land. It's nature's no trespassing
sign," he said, "and it works."

"It may work for *you*," I sputtered, "but then, it's a little
easier for you to accomplish!"

I don't know what I was thinking. I wasn't using my head.
Obviously I didn't have to make my no trespassing sign the
way the animals did. It took me a few minutes to collect my
thoughts and figure out a better way.

Having done so, I found myself trudging out to the campsite,
gear in tow and carrying—a little gingerly, I suspect—a small
cup. Once at my territory, I traced a circle in the sand with the
contents of the cup. Only as I was doing this did I see the
absurdity of it all. I laughed out loud.

And then, in the next moment, I had a more significant
thought. I am the desert. I am the animals I would fear. I am
the sky above and the wind and the air and the Being in the
midst of it all. I was trying to protect myself *from me*. I
realized that any animal that might come along would be my
own creation and would have in it the seed of God, and that
once I took dominion over myself the animals would be to me

whatever I called forth. Fear is what attracts that which is feared. I crawled into my sleeping bag with a new understanding.

The sounds of the desert at night are remarkable, precisely because there usually *are* no sounds. When they do occur, they are the only sounds. There is not much competition. If there is a sound in the desert, you cannot fail to hear it. In the middle of Los Angeles you can fail to hear a great many things. The acoustical interference from other noises is terrific. Have you ever had the experience of riding in a car and not hearing an ambulance siren until it was three feet away? In the desert, you'd have heard it three *miles* away. I am sure that it is because of this fact that the desert has always been a place for soul-searching.

I lay still for a long time. Then, hearing nothing and seeing nothing around me, my attention turned inward. First to the physical. I began suddenly to become aware of how my body was pressing against the ground through the sleeping bag, of where it was comfortable and where it was not, of the lumps in the bag and the humps on the ground. Funny, I thought, I wasn't aware of any of these things when I was keeping an eye peeled for strange animals and both ears tuned in for things that go bump in the night. Focus is an amazing thing; *it can totally determine your experience of life.* As you grow aware, you experience the seemingly smooth ground as humpy, when only a moment before it did not seem that way at all. This intense awareness reminded me of the story of the princess and the pea.

The Moment of Discovery

Soon I focused away from my body and the ground on which it rested and the earth became all smooth again. My mind traveled to limbo, to nowhere, to space. I thought of nothing and everything. And finally, after some time, I said, "Well, I haven't found myself!"

I don't know what I was hoping would happen, but whatever it was it wasn't happening. Then I realized I hadn't *asked* to find myself. I had been lying there in undirected meditation. Undirected meditation never goes anywhere—and an undirected life never goes anywhere, either. Nothing happens unless you ask for it and focus your energy on it. There was that old bugaboo again, focus. You can sit and wait, *but if you don't know what you're waiting for, it will never come to you.*

"All right," I spoke within, "I am ready to find myself." Then I closed my eyes, took a deep breath, and made the request. "Holy Father, reveal my Self to me."

Nothing.

I opened my eyes. Blackness. Then, as my eyes adjusted, the soft light from the heavens washed the silent scene in front of me. And then it hit me. "Oh," I said in wonderment, almost out loud, "I'm looking at myself." And in that moment the sand was me, the trees were me, the sky was me, the stars were me, the air was me, the clouds were me, and everywhere I looked I saw my Self.

I allowed myself to experience this feeling for a very long time. It was the feeling of oneness that many people have described—a feeling of unity and total identification with all that is. I am the planet, I thought to myself. I am all of it.

I sat there longer. Then I rose silently and walked back toward the lodge without another word to myself. Even inner dialogue was no longer necessary, for there was nothing to say, neither to myself nor to anyone else. I found my way to my room, closed the door, and went to bed. I glanced at the clock before closing my eyes. Ten past eleven. I had been outside nearly four hours.

• • •

Morning came as quickly as thought itself. I opened my eyes to find sun rays streaming into my room, greeting me with warmth and welcoming me to a new experience of my Self. I saw my own brilliance, my own glow, my own warmth in the shafts of sunlight, and even as the light touched me, I knew I could touch someone else. I awoke completely, showered, then, after a light breakfast, joined the others in the main room for more sharing.

Ramtha spoke to us of many things. And to me, in particular, he said, "Why do you do what you do?" I took a short breath. It felt like the talk show revisited. The question was the same, only asked a little more kindly. As at the radio studio, it caught me a little off guard. Even as I was thinking of how to answer, the entity Ramtha, who seemed to know everything, went on.

"You know perfectly well," he said, "that if you keep it up, the politicians will hunt you down and ruin you. The soothsayers and religious fanatics will have you destroyed. You will kill yourself in this way, because you will not be able to tolerate your life."

He was right. I did know this to be true. I knew it because it was I who had attacked those others, I who had judged them, I who had condemned their life-style. I had condemned the poor. I had condemned the rich. I had condemned the religious and the nonreligious. I had condemned everyone who did not fit my ideal . . . when I had not even become my *own* ideal.

I returned to San Diego and stopped everything. I said, "It's gone. It's no more and it's over."

6. Telling the Congregation

The building in which we were presenting our Sunday services in San Diego was packed on the morning I made the decision to announce my resignation. No one in the ministry knew anything about that decision. How could they? I didn't know about it myself until I awoke that morning. The day I came back from Yucca Valley I knew it would be only a matter of time before the old game would be over, but I had not decided when that time would come. Also, aside from my private conversations with Reuben, I had pretty much kept my own counsel about all of this.

I am not sure what made St. Patrick's Day the time (perhaps it is because I am part Irish), but on March 17 I arose knowing that if I had to keep on "keeping on" after the revelations I had had about my new life, I would be denying my own integrity, my own truth. I had loved my work. I had gained tremendous wisdom, and I had become greater in my capacity to love, to know happiness, and to have compassion for my fellow man.

But to be true to my integrity and my purpose I could not continue as I had, knowing what I knew now.

One can stand on the edge, but unless one steps off one never can fly. It was now or never. I knew I was traveling a fast track, and my momentum was increasing by quantum leaps. The reactions, publicity, and press attention were mounting daily, and so was the interest of radicals.

The thought that my life might end in the physical sense if I didn't get off my soapbox and stop agitating people was increasingly with me. Many people found what I was doing agitating because I was dealing with issues with which people do not like to deal. My messages were confrontational. People have been taught to live in little boxes; they've been taught to conform, to have one particular point of view, to have one religion (or at least one basis for a number of different religions), and to have a preset direction in life. They also have been taught to accept these points of view, religions, and directions whether or not they are leading happy lives. One must not stray from the norm, one must not violate the rules, one must not question the standards, and one most certainly must not propose *new* norms, rules, and standards!

I, of course, was proposing new norms, rules, and standards all over the place. I was a new norm, rule, and standard in and of myself! I touched daily on topics that no minister, let alone a woman minister, was supposed to touch on. These were topics at the heart and the core of people's unhappiness and anger and disease. They were the cause of poverty, war, and crime. I was telling people that I had the solution to these problems and advising them what they would have to do and give up if they really wanted to rid themselves of these problems. I was telling them to give up their current norms, rules, and standards! I was telling them to give up the path of scarcity and fear *and begin to love*, and that their love was going to have to be a new kind of love—*a love without condition*.

The healing process always involves agitation. There is always a point when one becomes agitated, because anger is the next step up from apathy, and what healing does is move you away from apathy. If someone wakes you from a bad dream, there is a very good chance that you will be in a rotten mood.

Some people do not want to be awakened from the bad dream. They are like sleeping bears. They would rather hibernate with the problem than have the solution. They would rather have the bad dream than the freedom (and responsibility) that being fully awake brings them.

There are people who cling to the norms and rules and standards of others for dear life because they don't want to think, don't want to make up rules of their own, and don't want to be responsible for the results when the norms, rules, and standards don't work. They will fight to the death rather than question their second-hand rules and standards, because questioning requires answering and they want all the questions already answered for them.

As if dealing with such controversial things were not enough, I turned out to be a very real person, a person who didn't act like a minister at all—a person who made changes and mistakes and acted outside the boundaries of conventionality. I was dancing to my own music, and this was unheard of. Ministers are not supposed to dance at all, much less to their own song. They are supposed to live lives of somber and gentle reflection, of goodness and piety, and be shining examples for the community. My behavior was not widely accepted outside the religious community, and within that community it was not accepted at all.

Don't get me wrong, there were people who loved me and what I had to say. The ministry couldn't have grown as rapidly nor lasted as long as it did were this not true. But there also were people who laughed at me, scorned me, criticized me, and, worst of all in terms of my personal safety, actually saw me as a threat to them.

The more exposure I received, the more the radicals—some of them religious fanatics—came out of the woodwork.

Those Threats and Lawsuits

One afternoon in the winter of 1985 I was home, enjoying a pleasantly warm San Diego day, when suddenly I heard someone shouting outside, "Heathen! Devil! Blasphemer! I'll kill you!"

I went to the front window to see what was going on and saw a woman in a red Volkswagen at the curb in front of my house. She looked sane and neatly dressed and her car was clean. Everything was normal except that she continued yelling these things at my house. I watched her for a while but did not go out, and before long she left.

I gave the incident no more thought until two days later when, upon returning home with Reuben, we saw the red Volkswagen parked in front of the house.

"Whoa! This is where we stop," Reuben said. "Let's get you to Rebecca's." I didn't protest. We turned the car around and drove to my daughter's house. Reuben returned to my house with my son-in-law, David, to find the red Volkswagen lady still in front of the place, ranting and raving.

The woman told them that she had come to kill me because I had ruined the reverse on her car and my voice was coming out of the drain pipe in her sink. The police were summoned and Reuben was very sweet. He knew what the woman needed was love and someone to talk to.

He was in the car quietly talking sanity to her when the police arrived. After being calmed by Reuben and perhaps frightened a bit by the police, the woman left my neighborhood, never to return. I'm sure she must have thought that, besides being protected by the police, I had two personal bodyguards who would make it very difficult for her ever to get close to me!

Clearly, a lot of changes were going on in this woman's life and she was projecting her fear and anger onto me. But this is not unusual, and I knew that it could happen again any time. If I had any doubts about that, all I had to do was read my mail.

Every week brought at least one threatening letter. I was never showed these because my staff did not want to upset me, but occasionally I was told about them or would hear people in the office talking about them. Some of the letters were more than a little abusive and very explicit in their threats on my life.

I began to be the subject of frivolous lawsuits as well. People thought that I had money or that the ministry had money and so named me or the organization as a co-respondent in some legal action for no apparent reason other than simply to do it. The fascinating and frustrating thing about how the law works is that I had to defend myself against these legal assaults whether or not they had any merit on their surface. I was beginning to see what happens as a person becomes well known.

All of the truths and realities about what comes of putting yourself in the public eye, particularly in a controversial way, were going through my head during this period. I felt threatened. I also knew that even if no one else tried to kill me, I would be killing myself if I went on much longer as I had been. We all begin to die in a very physical sense whenever we spend our energy doing something we do not want to do or *not* doing something we do want to do. My life was now all-important to me—more important than anything else!

Changing Values

What had been important to me was what the world thought of me and that I could prove that my point of view of God and Jesus and religion and life was valid. I was traveling the outer path, hoping that the outer world would acknowledge me as being a valuable person who made a difference—a person who was beautiful and loving and wonderful.

Now suddenly my priority was my own experience, my company with myself. My own feelings, my own truth, and my own happiness had become more important to me than doing another talk show, facing another audience, hearing another accolade, or receiving another material thing. I had found what I had been seeking, and it surprised me, because when you find what you have been seeking it turns your whole life around.

I went to the service that morning telling no one what I was feeling inside. As strongly as I felt when I awoke, I still am not sure that I would have told anyone if I hadn't been forced to in a sense. Nobody is forced to do anything, of course, but sometimes it looks as if circumstances move us closer to activating our own decisions. It is wonderful how the universe supports us once we have made up our minds. Life compels us upward and onward into more life.

The first part of the service played before me like a movie in which I had no part. I knew the script, of course. I had appeared in other versions of the same film, but on this day I didn't feel like a member of the cast. Yet there I sat, in what was easily the most prominent position on the set, in the white armchair reserved for the minister. I felt out of place. I wondered what I was doing there. I was there, but I was also weightless, high from an energy source beyond anything I had ever experienced. I was detached from everyone, at the same time feeling unified with each person in a divine, cosmic dance of love. Oh, how I enjoy being with great numbers of people in love! There is nothing like it! How blessed I felt that these people had trusted me and allowed me to be in their lives. They had taught me well!

The minister who handled the opening and closing of the service—the announcements before and after my talk and other housekeeping matters—was speaking to the congregation, doing his usual fine job. How I loved him this morning and felt his glory. I heard him say, "How many of you here had a chance to be at Terry's last TV taping?" (We videotaped our programs in advance, distributing them to stations across the country a month's worth at a time.)

A few hands went up. I knew what he was doing. He was enlisting people to come to the next television taping. I didn't want him to. I wanted the game to be over, not to get bigger. The time was now!

"Well, these TV tapings are very special, as those who have been there can tell you. And this is your chance to support Terry and the ministry in putting this word out to thousands of people who—"

I stopped him in mid-sentence. "No!" I said from my chair.

Standing there at the podium in the center of the stage, the assistant looked stunned. "What?" he blurted, turning sharply to me.

I said, "No, no . . . I'm not going to be doing that any more."

The interruption was as much a surprise to me as it was to him. I didn't know what to say next. I only knew that there wouldn't and couldn't be another television taping in the old way. I could no longer handle the pressure of constantly needing to enroll people. Whatever I did from here on had to be gentle, loving, and effortless.

The auditorium was absolutely silent. I glanced around and saw that everyone was looking at me, wondering if I had gone mad. I smiled broadly and plunged ahead. When you're on the diving board, there's nothing to do but jump in.

The sound man turned on my lapel microphone halfway through my next sentence. The people in the back and in the balcony hadn't heard our brief exchange, they only saw that something had stopped the service in mid-beat, and they knew that it had something to do with me, because the platform assistant and everyone else was staring at me. Then they picked up my audio in mid-sentence.

"—going to be talking about that later. That's all over with."

Perplexed, our minister of the day made the best of the situation. "Nobody ever tells me anything around here!" He grinned. The audience laughed a nervous laugh and all of us on

the stage—myself, the minister, and everyone in the choir—
joined in. None of us knew what we were laughing about, but
it felt good to laugh. It seemed to release the tension. The
minister told the congregation about the Easter Sunday service,
again encouraging and motivating them to show up.

As I look back I see that people always got tremendous value
from showing up at whatever I did because it was always my
intention that they receive great value. My sense of struggle
came from the thought that they *wouldn't* show up unless I
advertised, enrolled, persuaded, or talked them into it. I could
no longer operate that way. I had to be valuable to myself, to
love myself and know my worth. I was tired of selling myself.

Off the Diving Board

The choir, as usual, was magnificient, and tears came to my
eyes as I sat there and listened to the song they'd prepared for
the St. Patrick's Day service. I was going to miss the experience
of church, I knew. I was going to miss it a great deal. Loving
others is the greatest, and I had blessed myself the past few
years.

It was time for me to speak. I rose and started for the podium
as the applause for the choir built to a rich crescendo, timing
my journey perfectly, as I had every Sunday, so that I arrived
center stage just as the applause died down.

"Thank you," I said to the choir members. "What a gift."
Then, turning to the congregation, "Good morning!"

"Good morning," came the automatic reply.

"It's wonderful to be here. And before the message, I want
to just share a little bit with you about where I am and where
this ministry is, and . . . uh . . . where we're going."

I felt a tightening in the first two rows, where most of my
staff sat. They looked up at me curiously, expectantly.

"Easter Sunday will be my last church service."

An audible gasp went up in the room. I hadn't realized until that moment how much of a surprise this would be. While I had spoken to no one about wanting to leave, I thought that somehow a few of them might have guessed, surmised . . .

I imagined there were some people—those closest to me—who must have known what I was going through, what I was thinking, what I was seriously considering. Looking down at the sea of shocked faces in the front rows, I realized with heavy certainty that they didn't. Suddenly I felt very alone.

There was no turning back now. I was more than just on the diving board. I was in mid-jump, looking to see where I would land. I glanced down and made eye contact with the one person, sitting squarely in the center of Row 1, who smiled up at me. There were no smiles to his right or his left, nor anywhere else in the room. Jaws dropped, faces looked as if they'd been smashed by a hammer. I returned his smile and continued.

"I am called by my own spiritual experience to go into my own wilderness . . . and to go into my own time . . . to contemplate myself. And there will be a small organization called Terry Cole-Whittaker Ministries to fill orders for my tapes, and all my classes will be put on video with workbooks so that anyone can have them. Whatever else I do will come out of my time in retreat. It is time for the renewal of my soul. It is time for new direction for all of us."

I was making it up now as I went along. A lot of my thoughts were months old, but the specifics hadn't been worked out. Now I was working them out. On the stage. In front of 1200 people.

"From time to time I will be making new tapes . . . for those people who experience that as an assist in recognizing themselves. And . . . I will do retreats . . . and I may move to Hawaii—I am looking at that right now—for some of the year . . . and then for the other part of the year live in the mountains somewhere or . . . who knows?"

I certainly didn't. That's for sure. I had no idea what I was going to do or how my life was going to look in six months, or even six weeks. A restless stir rode the audience like a wave.

"We will have retreats," I repeated, "for those who want that kind of an environment. And then we will do tours from time to time around the world at different high energy points of spiritual enlightenment . . . for those who choose to do that."

I qualified myself to make sure that no one thought I was urging anyone to attend this or come to that or do *anything* that he or she did not want to do.

I glanced from left to right. No one was smiling. I felt I owed more explanation. I felt like a daughter who had come home to tell her parents she wouldn't be coming home any more because she was now going to be living with her boyfriend. It was that I-know-I'm-doing-something-you're-not-going-to-like feeling, combined with that but-this-is-what-brings-me-pleasure-and-so-I'm-doing-it-anyway determination that so often marks our youth. And, standing up there in front of the congregation, having just freed myself of it and my entire ministry, I felt young again.

"It's a wonderful thing to be able to answer the call of your inner self as to where you need to go and what you need to do," I offered. "I did the ministry for me. It was what I needed to do. It was my vehicle . . . to move me into enlightenment. Out of serving, out of sharing, out of teaching, out of going through whatever obstacle I created in my path, it has brought me to this point in my life. And I am now guided from my own inner being not to look back, but to move on . . . and . . ."

I took a deep breath. It felt as if no one else in the room was breathing and that I was doing it for all of us.

". . . I want to thank you for the experience . . . and . . . I am no longer a television evangelist . . . period."

I sighed. Was no one in the room going to make this any easier for me? Then, from the back of the hall, I heard a short, staccato "Whew!" It was a sound people in our congregation made when they approved of something, or when they "got it" in a big way. It seemed to release an energy, to open up the

room. Someone began applauding . . . then another . . . and
another. The applause rose to a deafening level. And then I
knew. They understood.

When the applause ended I said, "And now I am going to go
play"—a cheer went up, as if someone had hit a home run or
scored a touchdown—"and do what I want to do."

7. How I Felt and What I Said

There have been mornings when I judged my talks as good and mornings when I judged them as bad. This was one of my good mornings in church. All people who say things to other people in public are at their best only when they speak from their hearts and convictions. They are most inspiring when they aren't trying to convince us that their truth should be our only truth, instead providing us space for limitlessness. We expand and become more along with them in that moment.

This is how I felt on March 17, and I have decided to repeat here most of what I said in my message on that morning—not because I want to make my truth your truth, but because my truth may be a gift that offers you the opportunity to discover your own. And why is this important to me? Because it is through the expression of my individual truth that I define myself, that I decide who I am. You define yourself by what you honestly feel, say, and experience.

I am fashioned by my relationship with you, by my relationship with all things. Our interaction allows both of us to become greater. I learn from you and you from me. Even though my truth is not yours, it can add to you and inspire you to become greater if you will allow it. *Your truth does this for me.*

And so I choose now to present the body of what I said in my Sunday message on St. Patrick's Day 1985, because many have asked me why I did what I did and why I am doing now what I am doing, and not everyone who asks could be there on that Sunday in San Diego when I explained it all from my heart without regard to how my words sounded or how the decision appeared to others.

Here is an edited transcript of that talk, with a few alterations I have added as afterthoughts for more clarity.

This talk is about you, and where you are.

One who looks back is not fit for the Kingdom of Heaven. Because once you are on the path, you cannot go back. You can wait for a while, you can try and hold it together and play the game of the world, but one day it hurts too much to deny who you are . . .

. . . because you are the treasure, and all that you need is within you. Call it forth.

Within each of us is the seed of our Creator. No matter how far away we go from the Source, when we choose to go Home, the way Home has already been mapped out and planned. In fact, you mapped it out before you left. So the script was already written. Even the day of your awakening.

At one time I needed to know how to take care of myself. I needed to know about prosperity, and I needed to know about running an organization. And also I had a need to be famous and a need to be well known, because that was my desired mode of expression. I needed to experience that in order to complete whatever I needed to complete. Why? Because I wanted to!

What I did was to go fully into everything I wanted to do. And if it looked as if I couldn't do it, I knew that I simply had a thought that I couldn't, so I called upon my inner self through the Holy Spirit and allowed myself to clear any thoughts of blockages that I had and to give myself permission to be what I choose to become.

I used my life experience to release me from the fears and thoughts I had that I could not be who and what I wanted to be.

I went on this trek to love myself. I didn't know that at the time. I went the path of the world because I thought that by following this path, you could have the freedom to live as you choose in the world. The reality was that the more embroiled I became in playing a bigger world game, the less freedom I had and the more I felt pressed to achieve greater success. The organization had to become greater in order for me to have more freedom. I desired to return to the simple, yet I also loved to teach, write and inspire. What to do?

What I did was spend more time in meditation, more time being peaceful, more time simply "being." What I was desiring to find in the world I was finding within myself.

I desired more and more peace and less and less conflict and controversy. I found I was the recipient of people's anger, resentment, and fears as well as their adoration, love, and appreciation. It became more apparent to me that I was putting myself in a position to be a focal point for people's responses to the message I was delivering, and it wasn't comfortable any longer. Who would have thought there would be people angered by the message "You can have it all. You are magnificent and deserve love!"

The more attention I received in the world, the more love and the more anger *came my way from others. I was stirring things up as I had desired to do, because I knew anyone's healing process involves facing one's own anger, resentment, guilt, and frustration.*

· · ·

Armageddon is the battle within one's self between fear and love, with love winning. It was uncomfortable, to say the least, to be in so many people's process of unfolding. I wanted all people everywhere to awaken to their beauty, but hidden beneath my good intentions was the ego trip of an arrogant world savior. As I aspired to more love and felt the need to stop punishing myself in the world game, I began to awaken.

What I wanted was peace and love . . . and a big turning point came when I surrendered to Jesus and the Holy Spirit back about three and a half years ago, because I knew there was more and I wanted it. I have always been willing to do whatever I thought would bring me more life, more God, more of everything.

This doesn't mean that you have to surrender to Jesus. Not at all. It wasn't Jesus that made the difference, it was my willingness to trust in a higher power . . .

I have found that each step to awakening requires a surrender to greater ease, peace, happiness, and love. We give up struggle and the war going on in our minds for a more subtle vibration of joy. Often this takes everything you've got, because you've been taught that life is a struggle.

As I began to experience more and more bliss and peace and happiness, I began to say goodbye to the game called Save the World (as if I had a duty or responsibility to do so).

World saviors make you think they are doing it for you or for Jesus, but the truth is, they do it for themselves. We've all been taught that it's not fair to be happy until everyone is. Yet with such a philosophy, no one would ever be happy.

Save yourself.

The world is saved by your being saved.

Love yourself.

It was time for me to save myself and stop with the nonsense that I had everyone else's truth. My identity was caught up in the world savior act, just as my attachment to being Terry Cole-Whittaker was denying me my freedom. It's all right to do whatever brings you happiness, but when your life and identity is at stake, it is time to let go. We are greater than our creations. I had to let go of everything I possessed and everything that possessed me. This meant I had to go through the process of asking, What is it I think I have to have, that if I did not have, I would not survive?

You then start looking at relationships, looking at money, jobs, your image of yourself, at every element of identity that comprises you—your opinions, your belief system . . . all of that. And you realize that anything you hold onto possesses you. It drains you of your vital force, because you must feed it and it must feed you, so therefore you cannot move into other realms.

It took every bit of courage I had to step into this realm. I did it step by step, and each time I had to let go of something. And when

I found something I didn't want to let go, it would be taken away from me, because I already had set the force in motion . . .

Trusting in my own emotion and experience, I reached for what made me happy and brought me peace, as opposed to what brought me pain or fear. Now this is all totally opposite to the way this world is. *If you listen to world opinion and you choose the dictates of society, you will be lost—lost from your spiritual self. Yet you may need to do that until you experience whatever it is that is there for you, so wherever you are you have to know it is the perfect place for you to be.* And at any time you can wake up.

That is another thing that kept getting me—the thought that this is the moment, now. I claim my God-self now, in this moment, and I will do whatever it takes.

It is not in the future. You have to be prepared for total transformation, or spiritual transfiguration, in every moment. It cannot be later. You must claim who you are, declare who you are now! I chose to be a fully ascended Son of God, to be all that I am in every moment, fully alive and totally awake. I chose to be one with the Father.

I called on the Holy Spirit. I called on Jesus or Buddha. And then I said, "I want to know the other ascended gods. I want to move into other realms."

What happens when you step into the river and begin wading across—moving to the other shore, going to the other side—is that the reality of this world begins to change for you. The value in it becomes less and less. You say, "I could go to another dinner party." "I can buy another outfit." "I can build another house." "I can have another product." "I can get it all going one more time, and I can have one more success. I can hold it together a little bit longer."

• • •

The trick is to allow yourself one more time to do the very thing you think would make you happy if you did it one more time. Do that fully and completely, with every bit of your being. Then notice, when you are doing it, whether you really are satisfied and happy.

It's like saying, "If I could just go on a vacation . . ." Well, go on a vacation, and then regard yourself when you're there. Are you satisfied? Are you more whole? Are you more complete? Or are you taking the same being with you?

Look to see if you aren't living for the "something" that will make you happier. Watch out for that trap. I was going to build a million-and-a-half-dollar house, and have $18,000 a month house payments, to which I would have become a slave. Instead, I started to give away everything I had—all of my possessions, all of my things. It wasn't comfortable, but I needed to do it. In some way I needed to become common and simple.

I often had to breathe deeply during this time because each step of letting go brought up an older fear of not being enough, not being worthy, not being successful or valuable. I realized how important it was for me to be special. I had used every means to make me special. I thought, If I have all this, I will be worthy, I will be successful, I will be loved.

Having all you desire is wonderful, but being possessed by it enslaves you. Can you just as easily not have it? Or maybe more easily, when it comes to being true to yourself? Those are the questions to ask yourself.

Would people be with me if I were not the "well-known Terry Cole-Whittaker"? Would I get to be with the people I wanted to be with if I were a "nobody"? I had to face that question. I began to spend a lot of time alone. I was with my children more. I played, went barefoot, enjoyed simply being.

I even began to find that to leave my home and the quietness of my own meditation was an intrusion upon my being. I owed my life to no one, and there was nothing in the world that could give me the peace and the joy and the love I was experiencing in my own being.

I realized then that I didn't have to save the world, that my life was mine, that I could live as I choose. I didn't have to please my mother or my father or my children or the public. I owed the world nothing. The racket of the world is, "you owe others something," and when you buy that dogma you are angry, because all you really want is the freedom to express and to be, which harms no one. You need do nothing else to be happy but express and be, because Life Force Beings are fed by their inner selves. If within yourself you have anger, hatred, and revenge, you feed humanity *that fuel and that food: When you experience yourself as love, all humanity, all beings, all life is fed from the core of your being.*

It has been really hard for me in the last few days, because my mind would say, "You can have both worlds, Terry." But you cannot. Who would save the world and lose his own soul? Do what you do because it pleasures you and for no other reason, because to believe you are doing it for others is to enslave them and possess them. But it also enslaves you, because you are caught in your own trap and your own system.

When you decide to take the path to awakening you will leave people behind. But that is right, because they need another experience to complete themselves. What you have gained to-gether is complete.

So . . . even last night before I went to bed I called upon my being . . . because I love doing the television program. But also I noticed that what I need now is to know my Self—in the quietness of my being, to know Nature as my Self, to be within my Self.

There comes a time when you will have awakened your Self, and everything you need to know. All you need to do is call upon yourself, and you know it. Because everything is within you. But you must call that forth. You must demand that from your Self. You must want who you are. You are the experience you are looking for. You are eternal life. All that God is, you are. But you must claim it to experience yourself as it by being it. What you desire you must become by being.

When the Call Is Heard, Go Home

So that has been my process. And when I awoke this morning it was very clear to me. When you know what is right for you, when you know how you really feel about something, when you know what you really want, the only thing left to do is step out and do that or have that or be that. Your mind will say, "But what will I do? How will I survive? How will I live?" And it will go on and on. And what you do is say, "Thank you for sharing," and go right ahead and do what you want to do.

When you hear the call to come home, go home.

So . . . I guess that's my talk. Just look to yourself, to see if what you hold onto isn't possessing you. Some are possessed by alcohol or drugs, others by a relationship, a job, their money, their education, their social position, or their families. How many of us are ourselves? Or are we a carbon copy of what we thought the world wanted us to be? We are caught, trapped in our own system. We lose ourselves in our own creation. We created our bodies, we created our world, and we created our universe piece by piece . . . and then forgot that ours was the creative force. There is so much more out there simply for the asking.

So to go home, we have but to remember. God is always there as the supreme Father. In creating us he created his Son so he could see his own reflection, for one only knows oneself by experiencing oneself reflected. And you experience who you are by allowing yourself to experience God as your reflection.

You have to be very arrogant . . . and humble. You have to be willing to call your Self forth and know who you are. Without that, you are a worm of the dust, totally fear-ridden. But the thing that you fear you become. And that which you resist you become. Because that is what you contemplate. Freedom is contemplating your limitlessness, your glory, your greatness, your Sonship.

I am not your ideal and I am not your hero—you are! And when you lose yourself in well-known people or gurus or masters, which all of us have done at some time or other, you lose your Self, because then you do not own your Self. Others can inspire you. Let them be fully who they are and enjoy their dream. But when you lose your Self by making others more beautiful, more powerful, more anything, and you sit there and worship, you have lost yourself.

Worship yourself. You are the Light.

8. The Aftermath

I left the stage at the end of the service, my eyes glazed with tears of relief and joy. People were crowding around me, but what I really wanted was to be alone. Reuben appeared at the edge of the circle, and I held out my hand. He took it and we moved away from the swelling group.

"Well, that's it," I told him, "I've crossed the Rubicon."

The knot of people from whom I had thought we'd distanced ourselves started laughing. I whirled around in surprise, and then I laughed, too. It was a good laugh. A tension releaser. And now I honestly can say that that was the last day that I ever have connected the feeling of tension with the experience of telling the truth. I had many times before, but I never have since. I knew on that day that I would never again experience tension and truth simultaneously. I knew that it would be much easier now, this letting go, this declaring who I am and who I am not. It would no longer be a cause for fear. Announcing what I wanted and what I no longer wanted in my life was a big step for me, as it would be for anyone, particularly when there is a virtual certainty that there will be those who don't understand and don't approve—and particularly when there is no place to hide.

I wasn't trying to hide, but it might have been nice to know that I could have if I had wanted to. I couldn't.

If I had thought I could hide, the newspapers the next day made it clear that I could not. I had long since stopped reading newspapers or watching the news on television, but others naturally let me know what I had missed.

Normally, the top of page one in major newspapers is reserved for stories of considerable weight and importance. This is certainly true of stories that stretch across *all eight columns* of page one. You can imagine my amazement then when the *San Diego Tribune* informed its 131,000 readers on March 18, 1985, of my resignation announcement with an eight-column spread, including full color photograph, spanning its front page.

COLE-WHITTAKER TO ABANDON MINISTRY

The Rev. Terry Cole-Whittaker, high priestess of yuppiedom, says she is bowing out of her San Diego-based ministry to go in search of herself.

After eight years of preaching prosperity as a "divine right," Cole-Whittaker told her congregation yesterday that she now has "a whole different sense that people can live in poverty and be happy."

She said she came to that realization during a recent trip to India and that she wants to simplify her own life.

"I am going to play, to do what I want to do. . . ."

The article went on for forty-four paragraphs, more than I have seen the same newspaper devote to some presidential news conferences. And that was only the beginning. Over the next several weeks, and particularly in the period immediately following our Easter service, stories appeared in the press from coast to coast—from the Meriden-Wallingford, Connecticut, *Record-Journal* ("TV EVANGELIST RESIGNS FOR NEW LIFE IN HAWAII"), to the Los Angeles *Times* (" 'HAVE-IT-ALL' MINIS-

TER BIDS EMOTIONAL GOODBYE TO FLOCK"). Nobody missed it. Even the 4000 subscribers of the Nogales, Arizona, *Herald* read the news. If someone had told me a decade ago that my actions—*any* of my actions—would be reported in the Nogales, Arizona, *Herald*, I never would have believed it.

I mention all this just to show what we do in this world to other people and to ourselves. First we put people on a pedestal, then we get angry with them for being there and try to pull them down. We also make much ado about nothing, but we do it in such a way that we create plenty of drama for everyone concerned. Then we step back from the whole affair and wonder aloud what all the shouting is about.

Most papers chose to highlight the fact that our ministry had a financial liability at the time of my decision to leave, even though this had nothing to do with the life choice I made. Nearly every story linked my departure with this financial picture, as if to say by implication, "This is the reason she left, folks."

It was as if the creation of a debt by our ministry was an unforgivable violation of some hidden set of standards that applied only to us. Other churches and other ministries—as well as national and multinational corporations by the dozens—run themselves with red ink for years, and not only is nothing said about it, it is almost expected. When we suddenly found ourselves in the same place after ten years of operating very successfully, it was a giant no-no as far as the media was concerned.

Since previously I had made judgments about people and organizations who could not win their money game and found themselves in debt, this reaction was more than predictable; it was unavoidable. What goes around comes around, and this is never more true than when we send out negativity in any form. As the renowned doctor and psychiatrist Elisabeth Kübler-Ross says in all of her lectures and workshops, "Negativity breeds negativity."

Only United Press International chose to bring at least some

balance to its report, quoting my remarks at my final service a
few weeks later:

> *What became very clear to me in the last few months was that I*
> *could no longer be in religion because I love everybody. I could no*
> *longer attack someone because they have a different belief. I did*
> *not have everyone's truth. I only had my own.*
>
> *I've found that the more I've been interviewed . . . the more*
> *people didn't want to hear the message. Instead, they wanted to*
> *know what I thought about Jerry Falwell. Or abortion. Or school*
> *prayer.*
>
> *It became clear that if I wanted to play the game of religion, I*
> *had to prove that my way was better than everyone else's and*
> *that's not for me.*

Unfortunately, those paragraphs were preceded by seven
others, and, as so often happens with wire service stories, the
later paragraphs were cut from the article for space reasons
when the story was reprinted in the vast majority of newspapers that picked up the UPI report. Most papers had room for
the first few paragraphs only, and here is what they said:

> *The Rev. Terry Cole-Whittaker, who preached prosperity as a*
> *divine right, has resigned her debt-ridden television ministry and*
> *is heading for Hawaii to simplify her life and seek "a new, high-*
> *energy space."*
>
> *The four-times married, one-time Mrs. California told 5,000*
> *followers in a tearful farewell sermon Easter Sunday, "I no longer*
> *want to be a television evangelist. I no longer want to be a*
> *religious leader. I want to be myself."*
>
> *She said she was chucking organizational responsibilities to*
> *escape to Hawaii and "transition to a new, high energy space."*

I did not describe what I was doing as "chucking organizational responsibilities" to "escape to Hawaii," but I understand
that reporters have to use language that is as colorful as
possible. That this may not always present the reader with an
accurate picture of what is going on doesn't seem to matter.

The Monday after my St. Patrick's Day announcement I
remained at home, sending word to the office that I would like

to visit with the entire ministry staff—at that time numbering around forty—the following day.

Over the next several hours and for a while the next morning I felt suspended between two worlds, as if I had one foot on a dock and the other on a boat, with the boat pulling away. If I wasn't careful, I could easily be in over my head. I could drown, I told myself. Even so—strangely, perhaps—I felt no tension.

I went to the office and we had our staff meeting. I knew I had come to tell the truth once more and I felt only love. As I looked around the room I experienced only love in return. If anyone on the staff was angry, he or she either chose not to show it or not to show *up*. We talked then and shared with each other from our hearts. There were a few tears but no recriminations. Everyone seemed to view what was happening as an opportunity to move on, to move up, to keep going. I didn't want anyone stuck in the game called "Terry," and I told them so. I didn't want anyone living my dream instead of living their own. The true master is not the one who has produced the most students, I told them, but the one who has produced the most masters.

"Go then and be masters of life and sovereigns in your own realm. Live your vision with the same enthusiasm and energy and commitment as you have helped me live mine."

To those who had made my dream their dream I had a special word.

"Sometimes, people in a leadership position hold up a vision—a cause, a purpose—that is uniquely their own, and this becomes the vision—the cause and the purpose—of other people's lives as well. Or perhaps it was that to begin with; perhaps it was even the others who had it first.

"For those of you who now share my vision, know that this vision has not changed. The vision is the same. To me, what is going on right now is simply the next step toward realizing that vision. It is the next step for me, and it is the next step for you."

I glanced around the room.

"You know, I remember some of these same feelings, only on a much larger scale, when President Kennedy was killed. It was as if a part of us had left, as if the vision we had shared together could live no more. But the call of John Kennedy was to live the vision with him or without him, because he was not the vision, only one of many working for it. 'This is not the end of Camelot,' he would have said. 'It is only the beginning.'

"So what I want you to know today, those of you who have worked with me and walked with me side by side down this path, is that the vision that we saw together is not dying. It is living. Take that vision, which is your vision as much as mine, and live it and create it anew wherever you go. Spread its news far and wide and be a living example that the vision is real and that it works. Be the one who *makes* it work."

The vision of which I spoke on that day is a vision of which I will speak in this book as well. It is, as John Kennedy's brother Robert so eloquently put it, an opportunity to "seek a newer world," and it is an opportunity that lies before all of us right now, at this very moment.

The steps down the path to realizing that vision, as I have discovered them, make up the second half of this book. These are my steps, not yours. Yet if you draw any benefit from my experiences, those steps will have even more meaning. In the appendix I have included both some exercises and affirmations that may be of assistance to you, should you choose to venture down the same path or should you discover yourself to have the same vision already.

The path to realizing your vision is the Inner Path. It is not the outer path of the world at large, but the private, inner path each of us is traveling even at this moment, whether we are conscious of it or not. The trick is to *be* conscious of it, which is what the "consciousness movement" is all about.

• • •

During the period before this book was written I discovered what for me were the most important steps along the Inner Path. Those discoveries produced the dramatic changes that took place in me and resulted in the dissolution of Terry Cole-Whittaker Ministries. So be careful. This book could change your life.

This is it! This is the big adventure! This is what you have been waiting for. This book can help to set you free! The steps that follow will, if taken, definitely do that. They will set you free from everything that holds you, that binds you, that constricts you.

But a word of caution! Whenever you ask for something, you must understand that what you have now may have to disappear to make room for what you want. In short, when you take the steps outlined in the second half of this book, your present circumstances, situation, and direction may change dramatically.

Take a look at the direction in which you and your life are moving right now and remember what I have often said to my congregation: "If you are not careful, you're liable to wind up exactly where you're going!" Now, if that's where you *want* to be, congratulations! Don't take these next three steps, because they most surely will cause you to stop and think, if not turn around completely.

On the other hand, if you have a sense that you want some new direction in your life, the rest of this book could be of far more interest than the beginning. The beginning only told you parts of my story. It was meant to be a simple explanation of where I am today. But this book was not meant to be, and is not, my autobiography. It is a description of the process I've discovered to take me from where I am to where I want to go, a process I am still using to continue my journey along the Inner Path. I am sharing this with you because I believe that, while the path is different for each of us, the steps along that path are the same.

How can the steps be the same and the path be different? Just as easily as you and I can be the same and different as well.

The steps along the Inner Path as I have discovered them are:

1. Giving/receiving
2. Forgiveness
3. Guiltlessness

You may not find the last term in the dictionary as given here, but don't let that bother you. A lot more than your syntax will be turned upside down if you take these steps along the Inner Path to the Vision. Your whole world will be turned upside down. (Actually, it will only seem that way. In truth, your world will be turned *right side up!*)

Before we talk more about these steps, however, it will be necessary to look at the Vision itself, so that you can see where I'm going and decide whether you want to be there.

This is what the rest of this book holds in store for you. It is a journey together down the Inner Path; it is an Adventure of the Soul.

9. The Vision

It was a dark day, and that made it unusual, because there are not many dark days in La Jolla. It was May, and several weeks had passed since my last Sunday service on Easter. I glanced out the window of my top floor office and saw huge, gray clouds hanging overhead, ready to relinquish their accumulated holdings.

"I wish they would get it over with," I muttered to myself. "If it's going to rain, *rain.*"

A crack of thunder slapped the air. A breath later, huge water globules angrily pelted the window, almost as if trying to break in. Startled, I stepped back from the glass.

Hmmm, I thought, feeling a momentary shiver of surprise. I'm powerful. What I say obviously goes! No need to be alarmed by my own power, though. I am surrounded by God's unconditional love, and someone I love is always near.

The door to my office swung open, turning me around.

Reuben stood there, smiling. My shivers went away, and I quickly felt warm again.

"Did I startle you?" he asked solicitously.

"No," I said, "but the thunder did. And the sudden force of the rain."

"Don't know why that should surprise you. You asked for it."

Now how could he have known *that*? I asked myself.

"Don't you remember saying this morning that what we need is a good rain around here?" He smiled.

"No, I don't," I honestly told him. "Did I say that?"

• • •

As your steps along the Inner Path take you closer to the Vision you will notice occurrences like the one I just described happening all the time, and you will wonder what is happening. I went through a whole series of such experiences before I began to see what was going on.

As I became more clear within my being and more purified within my soul—through letting go of fears, letting go of old beliefs, loving myself and others more—I found that whatever I thought would manifest itself in my life, sometimes instantly. If I was apprehensive about something, the phone would ring and the very thing about which I had been apprehensive would be presented to me from the other end of the line. Or if I felt love and bliss, someone loving or wonderful would walk through the door.

I knew from my years of learning and teaching that these apparent coincidences were nothing of the sort. There is no such thing as coincidence; everything is cause and effect. Still, I was astonished at the rapidity with which the effect manifested itself.

After my return from India and from Yucca Valley, the pace of this "beingness" accelerated by quantum leaps, sending me on a roller coaster of self-expression.

That roller coaster took me before my congregation on March 17, 1985, to explain that there would soon be no more

ministry, and before my staff two days later to explain that the
end of the ministry did not mean the end of the Vision.

And it did not. The vision for which the ministry stood lives
on, precisely because it was not our vision alone, but the vision
of hundreds of thousands of people all over the world. It is the
vision of a New World in a New Age of Enlightenment, which
masters and teachers have spoken of for a millennium. The
time of this new age draws rapidly upon us. Indeed, its
dawning has already begun. You may have missed it, although
I don't really see how you could have, what with all that has
been going on around us lately in every area of human
endeavor all over the planet. One has but to look at the
entertainment business alone to see the shift that has taken
place.

The night before this chapter was written, a friend of mine
called me and said, "Terry, you won't believe what I just heard
on TV."

"What?" I asked him.

"There is a program called 'Kate and Allie,' which is extremely well written and which I've always enjoyed for that
reason. Tonight's episode was all about a little boy whose new
kitten had died, and Kate and Allie explain to him all about
death and the different beliefs about what happens to living
things when they die.

"At one point one of the women says to the little boy, 'Now
there are those who believe that there is a soul that lives on
after our bodies die, and that soul is nothing more than our
feelings.' I couldn't believe it. This is dialogue on 'Kate and
Allie,' and they're talking about the soul being nothing more
than feelings. That's what you've been saying all along, but I
never thought I'd hear dialogue on a prime-time sitcom devoted to making that point."

I told him I never thought I'd see a movie like *Cocoon* either,
or any of a number of other recent films that have introduced
concepts and possibilities of the unlimited into our conscious-

ness at such a pace and in such a way that many can accept them.

The energy pattern has changed dramatically in politics and religion as well. Science, too, has seen the impact of this leap of consciousness, and soon the changes brought about by this growing shift in awareness will permeate every social system humans have invented.

No, if you have been paying any kind of attention at all to the world around you, I do not seriously think you could have missed the shift that has taken place.

• • •

The vision to which others and I have so often alluded is growing in the minds and hearts and souls of men and women and children even now. Soon it will come into full bloom. The result will be the New World of which I speak, the New Age of which so much has been said and written and predicted.

To me this is not fantasy, but fact-to-come, just as what looked very much like fantasy ten, fifteen, twenty-five, and forty years ago is fact today.

If someone had told you in 1947 (presuming you were even living in 1947) that one day not too far in the future doctors would take the heart out of a dying person and replace it with the heart of another person who had already died, and in so doing keep the first person alive and, moreover, return that life to normalcy, you might have found it difficult to believe. And if someone had told you a diseased heart would someday be replaced with a mechanical one, it would have strained the limits of credibility beyond the furthest reach of your imagination.

When in the early Sixties John F. Kennedy called for a man on the moon by the end of the decade, it seemed to many that he was asking for the impossible. Kennedy's vision presented one of the boldest challenges ever to mankind's creativity and ingenuity, requiring all of us, in our thoughts and actions, to stretch past previous limits and prepare to create a new reality.

Only a few years before this magnificent feat was accomplished, the most intellectually advanced among us might have called such an event pure science fiction.

In the past fifty years we have seen mind-boggling advances in medicine, science, locomotion, communication, and basic technology, compared to what was considered at all *possible* less than half a lifetime before. It is within this context that one must consider the Vision for a New Tomorrow, once held by a courageous few but now held by increasing thousands.

It may be that what I am about to say will seem outrageous, outlandish, or, from some points of view, even blasphemous. To those who indeed see blasphemy here (and there will be some), I remind you of the long list of people, from Socrates to Galileo to Charles Darwin, who have spoken of things called blasphemous. They were not the first, nor were they the only, nor will they be the last humans publicly denounced for speaking of things outside the realm of current human consciousness.

Opposition and disbelief did nothing to alter the truths these men discovered nor the grand vision they presented upon which so much of our present experience of life and the universe is based. Opposition and disbelief will have a similar lack of effect on the New World, which so many on this planet now envision. Those who oppose such a Vision will, in fact, simply disappear, just as those who opposed other visions and visionaries long since have returned to dust, while the visions they so vehemently attacked live on.

The Vision As a Practical Healer

The Vision for Tomorrow, which is part of this book as well as of the consciousness of thousands upon thousands of people now working toward it, was most recently discussed and explored in a week-long retreat held in Maui in August 1985. The retreat was sponsored by the Foundation for Spiritual Study, the small organization with which I choose to work now that Terry Cole-Whittaker Ministries has been dissolved. I was facilitator for the retreat, one of a series offered by the foundation for people who wish to come together to continue their spiritual studies in an atmosphere of safety and support.

There were sixteen of us in the retreat. We talked for days about our concerns relating to the human experience.

I want you to join now as a member of that group. I want you to share our explorations and discussions on the Vision of which I have been speaking, so that you may decide whether you want this vision to be your vision—or discover that it is your vision already.

It began, as so many discussions do, over an incident having nothing to do with the Vision itself. We were in the middle of a rebirthing session on the second day of the retreat. Rebirthing is a deep breathing technique that allows many people to get in touch with and then release unwanted or unresolved emotions, feelings, thoughts, or memories and flush out old fears and restrictions. People lie down during this exercise.

As I looked at the room full of people lying comfortably on the floor I heard sobbing. Turning, I saw a young woman shaking with tears. She was trying to hold them in, but they would be held back no longer.

I moved to her and said quietly, "Let that go. Let whatever that is go."

She sobbed more loudly then, and her body heaved in sudden jerks that testified to the pain she was feeling inside.

I let her be for a moment, so that she might have the experience. Then I bent down to be closer to her and whispered, "What are you feeling?"

She answered me through her continued sobs.

"Guilt."

"About what?"

"I c-can't t-tell you."

She let out a dull moan and squirmed on the floor as if trying to make the pain or the memory, whatever it was that was making her cry, go away. It would not.

"Look at what it's costing you to hold that in," I said softly. She did not speak. "You're safe," I whispered. "I won't judge you."

She looked up at me with the eyes of a child wanting . . . needing . . . so much to trust.

"I . . . I . . . had an abortion," she whimpered.

I told her I loved her, and no matter what she said, I would still love her.

"I had . . . five abortions."

"I love you," I repeated. "And those other beings you started to create love you. Those beings got to spend the time with you that they wanted to spend with you, and then they moved on. You cannot do something to a being, which is pure spirit, unless it wants that done to itself. There is no death, there is only life."

She cried harder. And then she allowed herself to let go of all that guilt—guilt she had been carrying around constantly, guilt that threatened to destroy the *rest* of her life. She let go of it then and there, released it. In a torrent of sobs and tears it was gone. Whether it would come back again was up to her, but for now it was gone. She looked five years younger. Ten. Her face seemed to have been washed clean of all its tiredness, of all its pain, of all its lines.

This woman had been dying inside, but that wasn't enough for those who would condemn her. As far as they were concerned, her suffering was justified. There are those among them, in fact, who would want her killed . . . in the name of God.

I knew this, and so did she. It made me think of the kind of world I would want if I could create it myself—which, of course, I *could* do . . . which I *was* doing every day!

That started me talking—not right then and there, but later in the retreat, when the rebirthing had ended and we had gone on to other things. Someone brought up the idea of the so-called New Age and his vision for the future, and suddenly, flowing through me like a rushing river, words and sentences came forth, spilling on top of each other and pouring out faster than I thought I could form the syllables.

"The New Age? You want to talk about the New Age? I'll tell you about the New Age, and the New World in which it will be experienced.

"The New Age will be an Age of Enlightenment and the New World will be a world in which there will be none of the things that make up the misery of the world today.

"This is the Vision of which others have spoken and it is the Vision which we, here today in this room, have an opportunity to begin to create. We have an opportunity to create a new reality and to put an end to the old.

"Some of the things in this vision may be hard for you to imagine, until you think about where we have been and where we have come from just to get here—where we are today. We have the ability and the technology right this very moment to produce some of the outcomes in the Vision in our next moment—if we really want to, if we really care.

"An end to starvation, for instance. There is no need for any people on the face of the earth to suffer starvation. We have the food and we have the technology right now, today, to bring an end to hunger and starvation forever, if we would only choose to do so, if we would only care. Oh, we say we care, but we don't do anything about it, and so we remain impotent in the face of a killer that could have been conquered decades ago.

"In the New World of the New Age of Enlightenment, there will be no more starvation. It seems such an obvious thing to say, yet we still have not been able to achieve it.

"The New World will mean other things, as well.

"It will mean:

"*The end of sickness.* Scientists are close to taking us to the edge of immortality even now. You would be amazed at how remarkably close we are.

"*The end of war.* There will be no cause great enough and no point important enough to require us to kill other people. The meek *shall* inherit the earth, and by the meek we mean the gentle, the loving, the teachable people who are willing, at last, to learn the lessons of a horrible yesterday and apply them to make a beautiful tomorrow.

"*The end of money.* Half the people right now are moving to a barter system, and the other half will cross over sooner than later. I will do for you and you will do for me and we will share and trade things of equal value. And soon we will not even care what the value is, because we will realize that out of each of us giving from our highest expression, everyone wins and we cannot lose. The monetary system in this country and throughout the world is undergoing fantastic change even now as I speak these words, and it will undergo more drastic change in the next few years.

"People who are hoarding money, thinking, This is it! are going to be in for a dramatic surprise. In the New World there will be no money as we know it today, not because money in and of itself is bad, but because it simply will not be necessary. Those of you who do not believe this need only look back a few generations to see how we already have progressed in the move toward a no-money society. We would consider many of yesterday's uses and forms of payment cumbersome and out-dated today, just as we will consider today's use and form of payment of money needless in the New Tomorrow.

"*The end of government.* Everyone will govern themselves. There will be no more tyrants and no more organizations to tell us what is good for us and what is bad. We will govern ourselves in peace and love, and we will do so without difficulty because we will want nothing from each other that we cannot have, and no one will have more nor less than anyone else unless it is by choice.

"The New Age will mean the end of government, not because all governments are bad, but because government as we know it will be unnecessary. Those of you who do not believe this need look back only a short distance on the scale of history to see how—as oppressive as some government actions may seem today—we have progressed from the days of land

barons and feudal kings and even churches, which governed
our private lives and burned some among us for witches. We
would consider such government barbaric and totally unacceptable today, just as we will consider today's governments
barbaric and unacceptable in the New Tomorrow.

"*The end of religion.* There will be no more God of vengeance for us to fear, and therefore no more God-fearing
people. Everyone will have *found God within.* The New Age
will mean the end of religion not because religions are bad, but
because religions as we know them today will not be necessary.
Those of you who do not believe this need only look into the
past to discover religious practices once considered unchange-
able staples of society no longer existent today (e.g., no
commerce on Sunday, no meat on Friday).

"*The end of discrimination.* No being in the world will
perceive a difference between blacks and whites, Catholics and
Jews, men and women, or any category whatsoever. Categories
themselves will disappear as a function of social and economic
classification, so discrimination will not only be unnecessary, it
will be impossible. Those of you who do not believe this need
only look back fifty years to see how much discrimination
existed then that does not—could not—exist today.

"*The end of work.* We will no longer be enslaved in a system
requiring us to do things we do not wish to do in order to
survive. Neither will we have to do what we do for someone
else in the classic sense. Hence, that which we do no longer will
accurately be called "work." We will all do in the world that
which brings us our highest reward, our highest fulfillment,
our highest experience of Self. In essence, feeling this way, we
will all be self-employed, and those things that need to be done
by teams of people will be accomplished by just that: teams of
people, all of them self-motivated and working together coop-
eratively to make something happen. It will also be the end of
an era of employer responsibility for employees. In fact, the
whole concept of employer/employee and work as we know it
today will end, not because all work is bad, but because work as

we have created it will no longer be necessary. Those of you who don't believe this need only look back fifty years to see how much of the work done then is no longer necessary today.

"All of this—the end of starvation, sickness, war, money, government, religion, discrimination, and work—will come about as a result of the end of two other things that now run our lives: fear and limitation. In the New World now being created for the New Age of Enlightenment, fear will disappear forever and the only limitations encountered will be limitations voluntarily accepted in order to have a given experience.

"The first fear to disappear will be the fear of death, because we will be finally clear that there is no death—there is only life. We will also be clear that we cannot lose at any game and that we cannot be hurt or damaged in any way by the life experience. Once we are clear on these essential (and really rather basic) points, we will have eliminated the only cause for fear there is. Take away the fear of death, damage, or loss, and you have taken away all fear of anything.

"Our fears will not be the first things to disappear, however. Given who we are, we will always be afraid—until we make our limitations disappear. This, therefore, will be the first item of business in the New World. As soon as we banish our limitations—all of them, physical, mental, emotional, and spiritual—we will have unlocked the door to the Kingdom. In the final analysis, limitation is the only thing of which we are afraid.

"As most people understand it now, everything is limited. Life is limited, time is limited, money is limited, love is limited, everything we experience is limited. And because we think these things are limited, we want more. And we are quite urgent about it. We take all kinds of action to protect what we have and to get more of what we want. We hurt people and we even kill them in order to do this.

"As soon as we understand and experience that nothing is limited, that there literally is no limit to anything, all reason and purpose for war, government, religion, and money will cease to exist. And when reason and purpose cease to exist, the thing or condition itself will cease to exist.

"With the end of limitation, then, will come the end of fear, starvation, sickness, war, government, religion, discrimination, and any other negative condition. Your experience of life will move to the untapped frontier of your mind.

"You will begin to make decisions based not on what you have been taught, but on what you choose to experience and know. You will live for the feeling, because you will realize that feelings are everything; feelings are the prize. What feels good is what you will do, and you will do that in every case as long as what makes you feel good does not make anyone else feel bad. You will find it impossible to do anything that makes anyone else feel bad, because that will ruin whatever good feeling there might have been in the experience for you.

"It is this level of consciousness from which you will be operating and which will allow you to be totally self-governing because you will be totally self-aware.

"This is the Vision and this is the New Age and this is how the New World will be, and we may experience this if and when we choose."

• • •

The room was silent for a very long time. It was not a solemn silence, but a joyous one. The air seemed filled with love and peace. Finally someone spoke.

"I have many of the same feelings you do, Terry," a woman said, "but what makes you think now is the time for all this to start happening? And why do you suppose people are so against this way of life that they have managed to forestall it this long? I have my own thoughts on this and I'd like to hear yours."

I was excited by her question. This is what these retreats are all about, I told myself. This is what they are for. I created them in order to give myself and others a forum within which to enter into just such mental and spiritual explorations.

"I think now is the time," I said, "because we have gone to the limit of limitation. Little by little, fear by fear, we lowered our vibration to become limitation, and now we have reached the limit of that. We can go no further with that, and now is the time of returning home, of taking all our wisdom with us and moving on.

"It's time for the adventure—what I call the Adventure of the Soul—to quicken and for each of us to awaken and experience ourselves as whole and sovereign. This is all possible because it is who we are. You become more by knowing more, and you know more by asking for more.

"What is bringing us into this new time is our desire for peace, love, and happiness. In all the history of the planet, this desire has never been greater nor found in a higher number of people than right now.

"Even with this desire so great, I have found in my teaching that it is highly unsettling for people to give up sickness, give up scarcity, give up misery, and give up the systems of the past, because they have come to believe all these things were natural to the human condition. The truth is that it may have become 'normal,' but it is not 'natural.' There is a big difference between what is normal and what is natural."

The woman nodded as if she knew precisely what I meant, which I am certain she did, given her level of attunement with me, which was something I could sense and feel. I went on.

"It takes a daring person to give up sickness and give up living from doom and gloom. It takes daring to actually live from joy and to change your work so that you are doing nothing but adding to people's greatness.

"What is daring about this is that it brings up a dilemma. What will we do when everyone is equal? What will we do when everyone can create what they want when they want it? What will we do when everyone governs him- or herself, everyone loves him- or herself, and when everyone is happy, healthy, and abundant?

"Do you understand what I am telling you? When this is

how things are, *it looks like there will be nothing for half the world to do!* What jobs will be left in the world if all the people are able to take care of themselves? Do you realize how many people this would threaten? Half the world makes its livelihood and gets its power from the other half of the world, which experiences that it has none."

One of the men in the group spoke.

"How do you think the world is going to overcome that? By what means do you see us changing that kind of thinking, so that the world you envision—"

"Wait a minute. This is not the world *I* envision. This is the New World we all envision. Has this perfect world not been the vision of all humankind since the beginning of time?"

"Yes, I should imagine it has, but—"

"And is it not, at some level, your own vision right now?" I asked him.

"Yes, it's what I want, all right. I'm just not sure how we're going to get from here to there."

"That's what the Inner Path is all about," I told him. "It's about 'getting from here to there.' This is the path we're on, and if we take the steps on the path that all those who love the Vision have discovered—the steps of forgiveness, giving, and guiltlessness—I believe it will be impossible *not* to get there!

"I believe that the peoples of the world will be able to sit down at a table together—perhaps it will be a round table at that—and talk of peace and honor and a world where might is not right and all is shared and everyone is equal. And they will be able to do this because they will see and understand that the table is God and the flower on the table is God and the body next to the table is God and all that is is God. They will know that as God-Man, we are the reflection of God and we are God who reflects himself and then experiences himself. This time is fast approaching for the multitudes, and it is already here for many who have dared to step into that realm."

I told the retreat participants then that when, in my earlier classes and seminars years ago, I began to share this vision and even the words "I am God," some people were shocked. They thought it was blasphemy.

"The real blasphemy is to say that you are not God.

"To be God is to love yourself, to love humankind. It is to love the slum and the palace, the rich and the poor, the high and the low, because you begin to see that everything is the same; it just takes a different form, and no one thing is better than another.

"When you love yourself the world becomes your beautiful mirror, your radiant reflection. It always has been, but instead of reflecting hatred back at you and fear back at you, it reflects love back to you, and joy.

"As you live the Vision, you will see beauty in everything, even that which you once called sin. You will find that there is nothing you would judge, and you will discover that you have compassion for all. You will begin to see past lives and know that you yourself have murdered . . . and been murdered. You have done the most disgusting things and the most saintly things. You will begin to understand that God Is. God allows."

• • •

Once again the room grew very quiet as all of us contemplated this thought. I turned to the young woman I had comforted earlier. "There will be no reason for guilt and no reason for shame. We will all simply choose to learn what we need and wish to learn, and we will see our experiences as devices for allowing us to do that, which is how God sees them."

A young man asked, "How is this going to affect our relationships with other people?"

I told him what I thought. "In waking up, you will soon loosen your attachment to this world. You will realize that you can survive anything, for you always have and always will. You will cherish your children, and they will be safe and nurtured and allowed to become their own master.

"Each of us will be open to the music within our beings, and our creations will be awesome by our present-day standards and understandings. We will then have to remember the words of the masters who have gone before us, particularly one who said, 'Why are you so amazed? These things and more shall you also do.'

"You will lose your attachment to people and love them more. You will realize you can be happy with everyone because you love yourself. You will talk with total strangers, and you will love them as much as you have loved any lover, child, or friend you ever had. You will love someone else's child as much as you love your own. Jealousy and envy will be no more.

"All the meaningless importances that you have had will fall away when you live the Vision, and pain will be removed."

The sunlight shone in brightly through the window now in a sudden burst, almost as if on cue. A marvelous older woman, sitting near the front so she could hear but saying not a word throughout, spoke up quietly. She was spry, with lots of energy and always a ready smile; she had radiated good cheer from the beginning of the retreat.

"Tell me again about death," she said. And then with enormous dignity she turned to the group and smiled. "You see, I have a reason to want to know about that."

I looked directly into her eyes, so soft and blue and wise, and said what I had said earlier. "You will no longer fear death. You will go through the experience of leaving your body and you will say, 'So this is it.' And you will surrender yourself into the Light. Then moments will pass and you will realize that you are still conscious, still aware. And you will know that what you have experienced may have been that thing you once called death, or it may have been a temporary time out of your body, not a permanent leave-taking at all. In either event, you will never fear death again because you will be sure that it does not exist."

I turned to the rest of the group.

"This is how it will be in the new existence. This is how it will be in the New Age of God-Man. This is the Vision."

10. Blockages to the Vision

Therefore take no thought, saying, What shall we eat? or What shall we drink? or, Wherewithall shall we be clothed? for your heavenly father knoweth that ye have need of all these things.

But seek ye first the Kingdom of God, and his righteousness, and all these things shall be added unto you.

Matthew 6:31-33

"Hey, you're way out in space, lady."

The dark-haired man stopped me as I was leaving one of the last church services I presented, just before Easter 1985. I had been talking about the Vision for the New World then, too, and he clearly was one of those in the congregation who wished that I had kept the discussion to much more earthly and practical matters.

"I'm just trying to get through my life day to day," he said. "I'm not concerned about some magical, mystical world beyond the year 2000 and how things are going to be. I'm worried about how they're going to be tomorrow."

For the record, my sermon that day was not about some magical, mystical world beyond the year 2000. That sermon and this book are about your life and mine, *right now*—and *tomorrow*. I know, and readily acknowledge, that the vision I have just outlined seems very far away to many people—if indeed it is even desirable. Yet there are those who are living it or living something very close to it today. They are living in the absence of worry or concern or even recognition of the so-called negative aspects of life. They live as individuals or in communities, but wherever they experience life there is no pain or frustration or jealousy or anger or hurt or envy or sense of longing for what they cannot have. There is no fear of losing what they do have or anxiety about someday not having enough. They live in peace and harmony, love and acceptance. The outward appearances and conditions of their lives may not seem to have changed and may not appear that different from the outward appearances and conditions of the conventional lives of others. But somehow they experience life itself in a vastly different way, which seems to make them immune to the turmoil, illness, and unrest to which so many fall prey.

Who are these people? Are they "spaced out," as the man in my congregation suggested? Have they dropped out of our society and our world to seek refuge in some secret mental hiding place? Is their game plan simply to stay out of touch with "the real world" and, by staying out of touch with it, to stay out of reach *of it*?

No. Hardly. In fact, quite to the contrary. They are staying very much *in* touch with the world around them. They are getting along in that world so beautifully not by ignoring it, but by *changing it*. And therein lies the secret of this book. *The world around you changes when you change.* The world around you reflects *exactly who and what you are, who and what you choose to be.*

This is an important point for you to remember: Taking the Inner Path does not take you out of the outer world.

The man in my congregation did not understand that I was saying (and I take responsibility for not adequately communicating this to him) that I had spent a lifetime coping with the practical problems of day-to-day living and here was *my solution to them.* He thought I was proposing solutions to some pie-in-the-sky problems of social interaction on a planetary scale, while I was talking about *his life, right here, right now.*

My friend did not get the message I was sending because my ideas didn't look very practical to him. They aren't. They are no more practical than the thought contained in the biblical injunction found at the beginning of this chapter, the meaning of which has been lost or ignored even by those who still admire its poetic beauty.

Here, then, is the second secret I discovered while walking along the Inner Path: *What appears to be the most impractical approach to life is the most practical approach of all.*

This is not a book about how to get to Woo-Woo Land. This is a book about how to make your life work *right now, right here, today and tomorrow.* And in so doing you and others who choose to create the same life for themselves *will automatically be creating the Vision of which so many have spoken.*

When it began to look to people as though I had stopped focusing on the practical problems of day to day and started focusing on other things, I lost some of my audience—just as I suspect I may already have lost some readers who may have come to this book expecting to find a more conventional "self-help book."

The purpose of this book is to eliminate the need for you to read another. Because that is so, it will not read like any other offering you assistance in getting through life. One of the choices I had to make when this book was being put together was whether to write it so as to sell the most books or share the most of my truth. I chose the latter.

I said at the outset that this book is for masters, and I meant it. If you want a book that tells you how to win friends and influence people or how to be a success in life, or how to solve life problems and be happy, congratulations! This book also does all those things. But it does them in a different way, a new way—a new way for a New World in a New Age of Enlightenment.

* * *

Before discussing how to get from here to there, you should know that I encountered many blockages to living my vision and making my day to day experience the highest expression of Self I can create. I want to tell you about those blockages, so that you may avoid them. To do so I have to go back into my own story so that you can see how these blockages were self-created and how they impacted on and affected my life.

The Game of "Bigger, Better, and More"

When I started my own involvement in what many people call the "consciousness movement" years ago, I don't think I was much different from anybody else. I wanted to be "better than." I wanted to be the greatest minister and the most inspiring spiritual leader. I wanted to be the most beautiful woman so that I would be loved and appreciated by men. These are the things I thought would guarantee me everything I wanted from the world, the most important of which (I thought) was a mate, so that I would never be cast aside.

I wanted to be special and irreplaceable and indispensable. Perhaps you have wanted these things, too. If so, beware. This is the world enslavement program of which I have spoken, in which we seek to become separate and unique and different. This is the game of Bigger, Better, and More.

You can win the game of Bigger, Better and More, but it may not bring you what you think.

In my own case, it got to where when I walked down the street people stopped me for my autograph. But then I saw people begin to be afraid of me because, after all, I was "famous" and "special." People made themselves less than me; they gave me their power. Soon I began believing that I really

was more special than others. The only problem was that I
could never be sure if people loved and adored *me* or *who they
thought I was*. Then I stopped seeing myself as more special
(which was the truth of it) and stopped allowing people to see
me that way. I refused to let them give me their power. This
process, which had been ongoing for some time, culminated in
the spring of 1985, when I dissolved my national television
ministry. Then an interesting thing happened. Those who
thought I had more power than they had suddenly saw that I
did not—and left. I had nothing to offer anymore. But those
who never saw me as anything but equal from the very
beginning stayed in the space with me. I found myself surrounded by equal creators, and I was in heaven, with no one
wanting anything from me because no one *needed* anything
from me.

Of course, I was surrounded with equals all along. They
simply refused to demonstrate their equality in my presence
because they had decided in advance that I was "better." For
my part, I wasn't looking for equals, I was looking for "less
than's" so that I could be "different," "special," and "unique."

You will find that you are surrounded by equal creators who
want and need nothing from you—people with whom you can
feel totally comfortable, totally safe, and totally yourself from
the moment you end the game of Bigger, Better, and More, if
you are playing it. Only you know whether you are. Be careful
to take a really close look. The game is played so subtly
sometimes that the players don't even know they're playing.

If you *are* playing the game of Bigger, Better, and More,
keep playing it so long as you experience yourself winning.
Keep walking down whatever path you are traveling as long as
it is taking you where you want to go. You will do this anyway,
with or without my advice. Each of us gives ourselves the
experiences we want in order to remember what we have
always known: who we are.

That is the eternal question. What is life all about and who
are we? This book is leading you to the answer. That is your

destination, whether or not you read this book. You cannot help but get there, because "there" is where we are all going. We could not go anywhere else if we tried. Heaven is denied no one, and our experience of our true Self is the heaven we have been seeking. You can have that experience right now, in this time and in this place, or at any other time and place you wish.

There may be other stopping points along the way before you get to the place we're calling "there," but that's all part of the process of getting there. Each of us defines where "there" is for us at any given moment. For you right now it may very well be a new car, that dream home, your right work, or your perfect relationship.

I no longer want or need, and hence do not yearn for, these things. This is not an arrogant statement to the effect that I either have it all or am above it all. It is simply an acknowledgment that I have discovered a way to make the car I am using right now (and in every "right now" of my life) new for me; the home I am in, whatever home that is, always a dream; the work I am doing in this instant always right for me; and the relationship I am in always perfect.

My goals are now beyond the physical. I have chosen to seek the highest, most joyous, most complete and fulfilling expression of my true Self that I can create and experience in this life. The interesting thing about this is that when I do that, *all of the other goals and yearnings of my life are taken care of.*

This is what is meant by *Seek ye first the kingdom of heaven, and all else will be added unto you.* This is why my sights, for myself and for my world, have been set so high.

Should you choose similarly to raise your sights, into the realm of what to many may seem to be the impractical, you will place in your hands *the most practical tool for the mastery of life ever discovered.*

The steps to learning how to use this tool are the steps along the Inner Path. They are the steps I took in my life after I finally removed all the blockages I had encountered to living my vision. The game of Bigger, Better, and More was not the only blockage, it was simply the first I was able to identify. Later on I began to see entire behavior patterns I had developed that continued to obstruct my path to the Vision.

Patterns and How They Begin

A policeman was walking down the street in Los Angeles one day when he saw a drunk leaning up against a telephone pole. Approaching the vagrant, he said, "I'm sorry, sir, but if you want to stand here, you'll have to move on."

There may be more wisdom than humor in that story, because truly, that is the way it is in all of life. If you want to stand here, you've got to move on.

You cannot stand still anywhere. Not in your physical life, not in your mental life, not in your emotional life, and not in your spiritual life. The effect of life is growth. The fact of life is movement. And the biggest problem in life is that everyone is trying to stand still.

Worse yet, everyone wants everyone *else* to stand still.

Of all the patterns of life that prevent us from experiencing our highest Self, this is the most insidious and the most pervasive. I found this out when I first tried to make a real move in my life, and I have rediscovered it every time I have made a major move of any kind since. My move away from the ministry is an obvious case in point.

We live in a very nervous society. The motto seems to be, Don't rock the boat, while the question is, When will my ship come in? The news is that there is no ship to come in because we are all in the same boat—and if we don't start rocking it, it isn't going anywhere!

This book is about rocking the boat.

Nothing stays the same forever. Nothing stays the same for even an instant. Everything is constantly moving, constantly changing. Some of the biggest difficulties we create in life are created when we try to hold on, try to "keep it together," try to *stop something from changing*.

Think about that for a minute. You'll see that it's true. It's
one of the reasons I've so often said, "Stop trying so hard to
keep your life from falling apart. It may be falling together."

I discovered this for myself again in the spring of 1985,
beginning a few days after my talk with the staff of the
ministry on the Tuesday following St. Patrick's Day. At the
staff meeting, everyone projected love and acceptance, and I
remember thinking, You mean I'm going to be able to make a
major move in my life and for the first time there will be no
objection, no dissent, no one telling me I can't, and no roofs
caving in? I was expressing this thought two mornings after
the staff meeting when the phone rang.

"The roof's caving in," my secretary said.

"What do you mean?"

"A couple of staff people came in here today to tell me they
are suing for lost wages. There's another employee out in the
lobby crying her eyes out because she says she quit her job to
take her position with the ministry, and now that it's over she
has no place to go. And the phone has been ringing off the hook
with creditors demanding full payment of all accounts due.
Other than that, everything's perfect."

Within two weeks of St. Patrick's Day, many key people on
my staff were no longer with me. Some were asked to leave, as
I began the process of pulling back, of making things smaller.
Others must have thought themselves to be on a sinking
vessel. They jumped ship. What surprised me was how many
left feeling bitter and resentful. After all I thought I had
learned about life and people, I was taken aback by the depth of
some of these feelings.

I understood, of course. I just did not expect it. If I had it to
do over again I probably would give more notice to everyone of
what I was going to do, if only to limit the disruption. But the
decision I made was spontaneous and honest, and I have no
apologies for it.

For a while there I thought an apology was in order. I had

been so used to saying "I'm sorry" whenever I did anything I really wanted to do in my life that I thought I had to say it again. But I knew at some deeper level that I had to break the pattern of apologizing for myself and allow each person in my life to take full responsibility for him- or herself.

I was thinking of apologizing to everybody because I thought I should try to keep my life from falling apart around me when actually it was falling together exactly the way I wanted it to. I couldn't admit this, however, because to admit that I was getting just what I wanted—in fact deliberately *going for* exactly what I wanted—would make me selfish and bad. This was the real pattern I had to break, the mindset that had haunted me all my life. *Being good to me means not being good to you.*

That pattern got broken when I realized that *not* being good to me means I can *never* be good to you.

In the end, we must be true to ourselves. All of us must be. If we are in a relationship we can no longer tolerate, we have to get out. If we are in a career field in which we do not experience joy and express exultation, we must leave. If we are in an environment in which we feel we will suffocate and die, we must depart. If we are in any way unhappy, we must change the conditions causing our experience or we become slaves to those conditions. And we must do it come what may, or what may come could be a greater hell.

Life, after all, is an experience of the Self. The hell of it is not knowing that or not giving ourselves permission to act on it. The trick is to get the hell out. Literally. When you are no longer experiencing happiness, when you are no longer experiencing your highest self, get the hell out of your life even if you have to get out of whatever hell you are in to do it.

I am aware this comment may seem brutal and irresponsible, particularly if your life follows the don't-rock-the-boat pattern. Convention says that rocking the boat is brutal and irresponsible. Yet the greater brutality and the height of irresponsibility is to ignore the deepest yearnings of your own heart and the highest callings of your soul in order to serve the yearnings and callings of someone else.

Neale Marshall-Walsch, a wonderful New World writer and my friend of the soul, stated this with beautiful and utter simplicity in a limited-edition book he wrote as sort of a private letter to his daughters, Mandi and Tara, several years ago—*The Manditara Book*.

> *Betrayal of yourself in order not to betray another*
> *is betrayal nonetheless.*
>
> *It is the highest betrayal.*

Guilt, the Killer of Life and Joy

I returned to my inner world following my Easter service and refused to feel guilty about the decision I had made or about how other people chose to have it affect them. I'm through with guilt, I told myself. I was through with it a long time ago.

Guilt is part of the pattern that had been running my life at some level for many years. It was a major block to my life vision. After the resistance-to-change pattern (Don't rock the boat!), it was probably the most powerful pattern I adopted (and one of the most powerful we all adopt) in terms of its negative impact on my life and its restriction of growth and forward movement.

Guilt generally is accompanied by or preceded by a false sense of responsibility for someone else. Both guilt and responsibility for others are a lie. The truth is that everyone is responsible for their own feelings, their own decisions, their own choices, and their own outcomes. But I bought into the lie over and over again in my life. The pattern established itself very early.

I was four years old and staying with my great grandparents at a resort they owned in the Sierra Nevada mountains in

California. My mother was a single parent, working very hard as a waitress in another town, trying to support herself and her children. Besides me, the eldest, there were my twin sisters, Connie and Bonnie, and a sister, Joan.

Little Joan was being cared for temporarily by close friends in Pasadena, and I had been living with Nanny and Grampa George awhile to make things a little easier for Mom.

The sun was very warm on the day that I established my guilt and responsibility pattern, so warm that the ground caressed my feet with a special heat. It felt good, and I was running and playing and feeling wonderful—as wonderful as a four-year-old should feel. Then I heard the call from the porch.

"Terry!"

It was a short utterance in my great grandmother's voice, but it didn't sound urgent, just . . . well, cross. The way Nanny could sometimes sound. If I had thought it urgent, I would have run right to the porch. But it didn't sound urgent in the least, not even when the utterance came a second time . . . and a third.

"Terry. Terry!"

I heard it, of course. How much better it would have been if I could have said I never heard it. But I did. Clear as a bell. Nanny's voice, calling my name from the porch. I simply didn't come. I was too busy doing what I was doing. The ground was too warm on my feet. Just to be outside was too wonderful. I was having a great time. Why did I have to come in now? It wasn't even lunchtime.

She kept calling me and calling me.

"Terry . . . Terry . . ."

I remember actually becoming a little irritated. Can't she leave me alone? I wanna do what I wanna do! I don't want to have to come now!

And so I chose to ignore her. I chose to keep playing. Soon the voice stopped calling.

• • •

I knew it was wrong not to have answered Nanny's call, and I expected a reprimand when I finally made my way home in my own good time a few minutes later. But to expect a reprimand is one thing, to be subjected to a dreadful responsibility is another.

"Terry," Nanny said in an ice-cold voice when she saw me come into the lobby of the resort, "I called you awhile ago and you didn't come."

I looked at her. There was nowhere to go to escape her stare. She was a stern, stout, pioneer woman with power in her stare and power in her voice—a woman very used to having her way.

She said, "What if I was having a heart attack and could have died and you were the one who could have saved me but you *never came when I called!*"

Tears welled in my eyes and a sting settled in behind them. For the first time in my life I felt guilt.

I also felt anger. *Why do I have to be the one to save your life?* I screamed inside my head. *Why am I the one who has to carry you on my back and be responsible for your very existence?* Harsh thoughts, right? Yet these are the thoughts we all have, in one form or another, when someone else tries to make us responsible for them in a way that is unfair and unworthy of them.

So it was that at the tender age of four I felt both anger at having to live my life for another and guilt for having fun and doing what I wanted to do and seeing someone else hurt by that. I had the same feeling—exactly the same feeling—when I dissolved Terry Cole-Whittaker Ministries! The pattern had stuck for a very long time.

Patterns Reinforced and Enlarged

I experienced a death that summer long ago. Not the death of my Nanny, but the death of innocence. I became less of a child. I lost part of my joy of being.

There are those who would argue that it was simply a necessary step, a step into the real world that all children must take. For me, I see now, it was a step into the illusionary world. The real world, the real truths, were those I knew as an innocent child.

It's been said that we really don't teach our children anything. Rather, we *un*teach them what they intuitively know. I find it difficult to disagree with that profound wisdom.

Patterns such as those I have been describing to you are burned into our behavior through life experiences, which often have much greater impact than we realize. The seemingly minor and insignificant incident with my Nanny on a warm summer morning many hundreds of thousands of moments ago is but one example. These "minor" experiences are reinforced and enlarged upon by follow-up experiences sending the same message in a new way and with a new emotion added.

I added the feeling of fear to the feeling of guilt just a year after the Nanny-on-the-porch incident. Fear and guilt were irrevocably tied on that latter occasion, and they remained together as unified emotions from that day forward.

I was living with my mother in Bishop, California. As a single parent, Mom was feeling terrible pressures. I know that now. But at that time, at the age of five, I could see things only from my own limited perspective.

Mom was out. I was in the bedroom playing with the twins, Connie and Bonnie. Suddenly we began to argue. The argument went on for some time, and when Mom came home she was greeted by the commotion as she stepped through the door.

"Stop fighting!" we heard her shout. "I can't take it any more!"

We stopped arguing, but it was too late, Mom's homecoming had been ruined. She'd walked into a battlefield.

Her day at work had been stressful. Her life in general was hectic. She didn't need another symphony of disharmony at home, of all places, the one spot where she hoped to find some peace and quiet. As I've said, I can appreciate all this now. And because I can appreciate the state of mind she was in when she said what she said next, I can understand why she said it.

I could not understand it then.

"I can't handle all of you together!" she shouted, marching into the room. She turned abruptly, looking straight at me. "I'm going to send you back to Nanny's!"

I froze. Something inside me convulsed. Then I pleaded with her. Desperately.

"Please don't send me! Let me stay. I'll be good, I promise! I'll be quiet! I'll never fight any more! Never, ever! And . . . and . . . I'll get a job! That's it! I can *help* you! You'll see! I'll do anything. Anything! Please don't send me, Mommy, please!"

The expression on my mother's face changed abruptly. It got softer, and the anger was replaced by some inner pain. She reached out, pulled me to her, and held me very close. I can smell her perfume to this day. "Oh, darling," she sobbed, "I didn't mean it. Mommy was just upset. Please don't cry. It'll be all right. You don't have to go *any*where. You're going to stay right here with your Mommy . . ."

• • •

A few days later a little girl appeared at a women's dress store in town. "Can you use some help in this shop?" she asked a lady behind a counter who seemed to be in charge. "Why, yes we can!" the lady said. "Landsakes, I believe every store in Bishop is short of help these days. Why, do you know of someone who could work here?"

"I sure do!" the little girl nodded seriously, then, turning toward the door, she said, "I'll bring them right in as soon as I can!"

"Good!" the lady smiled.

It wasn't long before the little girl returned. "Hello," she said brightly to the lady behind the counter. "I brought your help!"

"My, you have come back, haven't you!" the lady beamed, charmed by the little girl's smile, as hundreds of thousands would be years later. "But where are the helpers?"

The little girl looked puzzled. It hadn't occurred to her that three-and-a-half-year-old twins could not be seen over the counter.

• • •

Wanting to take the burden from others became part of my pattern for the rest of my life. It is why I decided to become a "savior." I knew I could shoulder the responsibility. I could deal with it. And if I dealt with it, whatever "it" was, that meant that I could stay.

If I "handled it," you would want to be with me. You would not send me away . . .

• • •

I've told you these stories so that you might learn how many such patterns become established in the first place, perhaps in your life, too.

Resistance, guilt, and fear are only a few of the life patterns that can rob us of our ability to create and experience our highest selves.

Fear As a Block to the Vision

Dr. Elisabeth Kübler-Ross, who wrote the world-famous book *On Death and Dying* in 1969 and has written seven other books since, travels around the globe every year presenting week-long residential programs that she calls Life, Death and Transition Workshops. She says, "Fear and guilt are the only enemies of man."

I agree with her. All of the other negative patterns of life are but derivatives of these two. Dr. Kübler-Ross also says in her workshops and lectures that death does not exist and that once you are not afraid to die, you are not afraid to live. Again, we are in total agreement.

Death means limitation and limitation is what people fear most. If people thought there was no such thing as death and that we actually exist forever, very few of the things they hold important today would be important any longer. They would see the experience of this life on earth in a whole new context, which would erase bigotry, jealousy, guilt, anger, war, and the whole win-loss cycle that creates negative experiences. In short, they would live the Vision.

Dr. Kübler-Ross bases her statement regarding the nonexistence of death on what she says are hundreds of cases of near-death experiences that have come to her attention in decades of work in the field of death and dying. In these cases, persons who have suffered what has been termed "clinical death" have "returned to life" to talk about it. Dr. Kübler-Ross reports that they tell remarkably similar stories.

Raymond Moody, another pioneer practitioner in this area, has published a book (*Life After Life*) in which he recounts many such cases.

Whether or not there is a life after death is not the point of this chapter. The point here is that people are afraid of life because they are so afraid of death.

Self-Judgment: The Final Barrier

Following fear, guilt, and resistance (resistance to change is resistance to life, which is resistance, period), the fourth obstacle or blockage I encountered as I sought to travel the path to my vision was my own self-judgment.

In many ways, this was my final barrier. In some ways it was the biggest. My thoughts about myself, I have found, are the most important thoughts I have. They form the foundation of my experience of life.

My lifelong pattern of self-judgment never came up in any of my life circumstances (although it came up in all of them) as much as it did in relationships. After years of examining my own behavior, I saw that whenever I was in relationships (and I nearly always was) I was continually looking at myself and judging what I saw. Then, after I judged myself, I would feel that the person with whom I was in the relationship couldn't possibly love me, certainly couldn't *keep* loving me, because I was not beautiful enough or intelligent enough or whatever.

My judgment of self then escalated into judgment of others. First I would judge the person or persons I thought to be better than I was. I would be furious with them for being what I was not. Then I would judge the person I was with. How dare that person make me not enough? In these moments I would separate myself from God and love. I separated myself from self-love as well as from love for the person I thought was better—to say nothing of love for the person I was with, because I was certain my partner in relationship would agree with me that the other person was more worthy than I!

Now isn't this an interesting pattern? Almost laughable, right? Interesting and laughable or not, it is hardly unusual. I have seen it a hundred times in others during my years of counseling as a minister.

In one of those counseling sessions someone once asked me, "But what about when your mate makes a remark that *is* judgmental, such as, 'You're too fat,' or 'Why can't you relax and have more fun, like Mary?' How can you call that judging yourself?"

"Simple," I answered. "If you hadn't made the same judgment about yourself already, your mate's words would have no meaning and would make no impact. If those words hurt you, it means you have already said the same thing to yourself. You're hurt and angry because your mate *agrees with you.*

"The remark becomes a mirror that validates everything you are feeling about yourself. You set up the mirror by separating yourself and comparing yourself and invalidating yourself, and your world is now attacking you."

I found that in my relationships I was manipulating people to get them to say they loved me and needed me and to feel guilty for judging me. Then if I felt pain and hurt when I judged myself, they could feel it, too. I could even make them the *cause* of it. I could become angry with them and say 'Who needs this?' and start looking for validation of my being from the outside world.

But the world outside cannot bring you validation of something you do not see within yourself. Even when you receive such validation, you will not believe it.

Clear Away the Obstructions!

I know of only one way to follow the Inner Path, to create and live your vision. The first step is to eliminate life patterns of resistance, guilt, fear, self-judgment—and any others that do not serve you. You know your own behavior, and if you look at it closely enough you will see these patterns, just as I saw the "savior pattern" I was following and stopped it. Some exercises to assist you in seeing these patterns and in eliminating them will be found in the appendix.

Obstructions along the Inner Path can be eliminated in one moment, in what I call the Holy Instant, through the experience of at-one-ment.

At-one-ment is, in a single word, what the Vision is all about. It is what life is all about, and no matter what you want in your life, whether it is a new car or a new world, at-one-ment is the way to get it.

The three major steps down the Inner Path are the fastest way I know to achieve at-one-ment. They are the answer to the question I heard repeated from my first day in the ministry to my last—and hear even now in the retreats and seminars sponsored by the Foundation for Spiritual Study:

"Terry, I want a better life, I want a happier experience, I want love without condition and peace and joy and abundance and all the things you speak of, but *how can I get from here to there?*"

11. Step One on the Inner Path: Giving/Receiving

*So let every one of you according to the gift he
has received from God, minister the same to your
fellow men, like good stewards of the manifold
grace of God.*

1 Peter 4

The suit looked marvelous in the window and I guessed it would look even better on me. I knew that I wore clothes well. I sighed, looked at the ensemble one more time, and walked away.

There was no point in thinking about buying it. I had $43.87 in my handbag. Don't ask me how I knew. A woman always knows how much money she has. Maybe it comes from counting pennies for so long.

Actually, it didn't matter what I had; I couldn't have spent it anyway. It was the grocery money. Oh, I could have got away with $1.50 for a pair of hose or $1.95 for a good paperback book, and no one would have said anything or cared. But $96 for a wool-blend suit? Not on your life.

You see, it wasn't my money. It was my husband's.

There was no such thing in my life as *personal* money at the age of twenty-three. Sure, I was an adult, married and the mother of two children, but that had nothing to do with it. I lived under the benevolence of my husband, and my personal money came from whatever I could squeeze out of the food budget. If I wanted something special, I asked him for it. The decision of whether or not we could afford something was not mine to make—unless my answer was no.

This is how it was for me as a housewife in La Cañada, California, a small community in the hills just outside Pasadena, in the early 1960s. I don't imagine it was very different for most other housewives then.

Maybe that's why the little church at La Crescenta, also near Pasadena, attracted me. Its teachings were metaphysical, and the first time I went there I felt that I'd come home. "Thoughts create, and you create your own reality," the minister said that Sunday. "Life is not a game of chance. There is no hell to which you can be condemned, and there is nothing and no one outside of you more powerful than you—not a god or priest or minister or rabbi or president or king or queen or husband [Keep going, I mentally urged him, I'm afraid of everyone you've named] or banker or insurance salesman or anyone at all."

I decided to go back the following week. And the week after. And the week after that. Soon I was a regular. It became my church.

This was not the first time I'd been exposed to such concepts. Those seeds were planted when I was seventeen. That is when I first recognized, through Religious Science (the teaching of Ernest Holmes), that God is everything, that I am one with God and that God is in me. It was at that time that I began to awaken, but it was to be six years before I began to go to church more regularly.

I went to La Crescenta and heard how wonderful I was— "You are God's perfect creation," the minister would say— then went home to a relationship in which I was insecure, feeling unloved and unappreciated. It wasn't my husband's fault. It wasn't anyone's fault. It was just where I was in my awakening. As I now look back, I see that I needed the wisdom of that experience so that I could have compassion for others in similar situations.

Not long after I began making La Crescenta my regular Sunday morning stop, the church began a series of lessons on prosperity. I had to laugh. The sermons couldn't have been more appropriate. I had nothing of my own. I was living life as an extension of my husband, and I thought that if he "had it," then I could "have it," except even then I didn't feel worthy to have what he earned because, after all, *he* earned it. I was there and had what I did have because of his "generosity."

These were my thoughts, these were my feelings at the time.

And, of course, there was always the fear that if he found someone more attractive to him, he would not want me.

I began to look at the job market one day, maybe in desperation, because of the thoughts I was having, and I saw in the workplace of the world a dead-end path to boredom and restriction. It seemed as if going to work would be a denial of my freedom and identity, not a pathway to it, because I had to do what I was told to do, rather than create my own life daily.

The one advantage to being a housewife was that at least I could do what I wanted to do. I could be with my children, who were my playmates—the little people I had decided to bring forth so that I would have someone alive enough to play with, someone to love completely, someone with whom *I* could be a child again. Why do we give up childhood, only to replace it with struggle and a step-by-step trek to the grave? This was a question I began to ask myself . . . and I began to awaken. I knew there must be another way to experience life, and I wanted it.

My children became my teachers. They taught me so much whenever I would let them. And they became my salvation, because they were the beings I chose to play with much of the time, rather than the adults of the world.

Yet I continued to wonder how I could experience the

abundance I was hearing about in church—and what that abundance really was. Would I have to make my husband abundant first? I was so used to everything coming through him. But he didn't like any of my ideas, and I began to feel as though I couldn't move, couldn't go anywhere with my life, because we were tied together.

Abundance began to mean the freedom to be me. As I explored this concept, I found it to be one shared by many others. Most people believe that if they were rich and powerful there would not be anyone who could determine their future or control their existence; they could create it in their own way. Most of us want to be cut loose from the bondage of the world.

When you have money, I told myself, you become the master of the material world. If things are not working in your life, you have the means to change them to suit you. If you have enough, no one can tell what you can or cannot be or do.

What I didn't know at the time is that life will always mirror where *you* are, whatever your net worth—which is, no doubt, why it took me nearly five years even to get the message about prosperity.

I was, however, gaining the courage to express myself. I decided that I wanted to start singing, something I'd always liked to do. With the help of a girlfriend who played the piano, I started creating my own little shows. I made some costumes and scenery and sent out flyers about us, and before long we were being hired by women's clubs and church groups. We were making only a few dollars an appearance, but each booking also represented a day of liberation and fun. I had the freedom to be myself!

We played these little dates in and around Pasadena and elsewhere in Southern California for several years. Now, at least, if I saved my money from three or four shows I could get things like that suit in the window. I started buying little extras for my children and house and for myself. It felt great!

My marriage wasn't the best during this period. It seemed to get worse. The more I did, the more I ventured out, the more I put myself first, the more resistance and criticism I received. But I couldn't let that stop me. I had had a taste of what it was like to have a life of my own, and I couldn't turn back.

I was making a transition. I could feel it and my husband could feel it, too. I wanted to own more of my Self. I had never been this way before, and it was not what my husband had bargained for. Just because I'd been elected freshman class president the end of my first semester in college, and later became homecoming queen, didn't mean that I was supposed to follow through with this beautiful-and-active-young-lady routine.

My husband made it clear that putting together my own show, actually taking it on the road, and then talking about generating my own source of extra income overstepped the boundaries.

I was stretching out into unknown territory during this period, and it was frightening for both of us. We expressed that fear in arguments, tears, threats, and general unhappiness together. We each had based our self-image on the other person and those images were coming apart.

• • •

A turning point came in my life when I was twenty-nine. My friend and I traveled to San Diego to perform for a women's club. When we arrived we saw badges pinned on some of the women. *Mrs. Alabama,* one said. *Mrs. Maryland,* read another.

I turned to my friend, "What is this about?"

"Darned if I know."

"Let's find out."

"Oh, they're all contestants," responded the first more-or-less-official-looking person we asked.

"Contestants?" my friend's eyebrows raised. "In what?"

"Why, in the Mrs. America Contest, of course." She explained that it was a contest to evaluate homemaking and family skills, as well as highlight the esthetic that complemented those skills.

My heart skipped a beat. Why, I could do that, I thought. I love the *creative* part of family life. I could be one of those contestants! I asked about the entrance deadline, was told there was still time, and made up my mind to get into the running.

• • •

I jumped at the chance to get into the contest because I had been thinking lately that maybe I'd been going about things the wrong way. Perhaps the trick was not to create ways to make money, but to create opportunities to express myself. Could it be possible that out of the free expression of self, money would come naturally?

I found out where to send for an application to enter the contest, wrote for one, and received it a week later. I was shocked. The application form contained a place where my husband was supposed to sign. *He had to give me permission!*

At first I was depressed and let down. I didn't think my husband would sign, since he wanted me to stay home, not go gallivanting off to enter a contest. It did not seem right that I had to ask him to do so.

Finally I said to myself, "Nothing is going to stop me! I have a *right* to do what I *want*, and I have a right to do it *without asking*!

I forged my husband's signature and sent in the form. I did not tell him about it until weeks later, when I learned I had been selected as one of the finalists. Among other things, the application contained essay questions to answer—How would you describe your philosophy of life? How will you raise, or are you raising, your children? etc. It also included a background information sheet that would have made an FBI agent blush.

I knew the fact that I had been homecoming queen and

freshman class president in college didn't hurt. And I answered the essay questions in my own way, being myself, and I knew the answers were thought-provoking and stimulating.

I wasn't surprised when I was selected as a finalist, but now I had to find a way to tell my husband! The competition where I had to appear lasted three days and was not in my city!

I brought it up one evening after dinner.

"Uh . . . honey?"

"Yes?"

"Guess what we won."

"Won? We won something? What?"

"An all-expenses-paid trip for two to Concord, California, for three days! What do you think? Can you take the time off? Can we go?"

"An all-expenses-paid trip to Concord! Who the hell goes to Concord? And how'd we win it, anyway?

"Well . . . I entered a contest."

"What kind of contest?"

"Oh, just a little contest for homemakers. You know, they do these things. Anyway, we got a letter that I am a finalist, and the finalists all get three days, all expenses paid, in Concord, where the competition is held. Isn't that great?"

I held my breath.

"Well, when is it?"

"In June. Here, here's the letter. Here are the dates."

I held my breath again. If he didn't go, or if he didn't let me go, I didn't know what I was going to do.

That's not true. I knew exactly what I was going to do.

"You entered this? You're a finalist for *Mrs. California*?"

"Yes. Pretty funny, huh? I didn't know I'd get to be a finalist, of course. I just entered it on a lark."

"What is this, a *beauty* contest?"

An odd look crossed his face. I could see he didn't like the idea of my prancing across a stage in a bathing suit.

"No, no, no. It's a contest for homemakers. You know,

housewives. They're looking for people with cooking, sewing, and homemaking talent. If I win, I get a whole new outfit, and we get an expense-paid trip to Minneapolis for ten days!"

"Hmmm."

After a little more discussion (can coaxing be called discussion?), it was all settled. We were going to Concord!

Out of the House and into the World

At the close of the competition, I was named Mrs. California.

Now I had a chance to go all the way to the national title. The best part about it was that I didn't have to do anything. All I had to do was be myself.

I had to share my talent, of course—they *required* me to sing in front of large audiences!—and I had to display my homemaking skills, and I had to get dressed to the nines.

In short, *I died and went to heaven*

Better yet, I *lived* and went to heaven. Heaven is when you're living your dream, living your vision, living the life you've been dying to live! I felt as if I'd been let out of a cage. I experienced myself as a separate person, having a life of my own, apart from my husband. I was acknowledged for *being me*!

It was a new experience for me to be going to a faraway city. More than that, it was a whole new revelation to realize that I was the reason for the trip, that I was the center of attention. It seemed a miracle.

Most people can't imagine living the life they've always dreamed of. I couldn't either, until I realized that life is a process of *self-expression*, and that only through my expression of the most and the best in me was I going to get what I wanted. Life begins when the dream ends, because that's when we stop *thinking* about something and start *doing* it.

Thinking about it helps. What your mind conceives your actions create. But if thinking about it is all you do, if you are not willing to take the first step on the path, it may take a very long time to get where you want to go, if you ever do.

I was soon on my way to Minneapolis for ten days of competition with women from every other state in the nation. Like me, they were all great participators. I remember thinking the first time I saw them, These women are doing the same thing I am. They're getting out of the house, getting into the world, finding a way to do something they love to do and being acknowledged for it.

I began to visualize and think of myself as a winner. I actually *felt* myself winning. *Feelings* are the utensils of God. They are the keys to the kingdom. Everything we do we do for the feeling, and the feelings we project are the feelings we continue to experience.

I knew I wanted to win whatever prize would give me the freedom for which I longed. I didn't really care so much about the title. I did sense, however, that something important could happen here, something important to the rest of my life. This could be a springboard, I mused. This could be it.

Somehow I didn't think I actually would go all the way. I felt, Well, I can't be Mrs. America because I've got an unhappy marriage and they'll find out. That would just blow the whole thing, particularly since I sang "I'm in Love with a Wonderful Guy" for the talent competition!

Then I got angry. I thought, Hey, why should I be penalized and not be allowed to be who I am because I have a husband who is reluctant to go along with possibilities? Why should I be penalized because it looks like my marriage is somehow failing because it doesn't fit the system?

This was the first time I was struck with a feeling that became part of my philosophy for the rest of my life—that I have a right to exist and live, even if my life doesn't fit some kind of world ideal or world standard of what is *worthy* and merits acknowledgment. I also began to realize that my need to express and live was *greater than my need to conform.*

Through all this my husband was communicating to me

what a failure I was. Maybe that was his way of motivating me. I don't know. All it produced in me was sadness. I felt that I had no adult who believed in me, no one who would support me. Yet, during the ten-day pageant I lay down on my bed every night and felt myself a winner in the competition.

"I am a winner. I am somebody," I would repeat to myself. I had to overcome all the feelings of failure and loss and rejection that I had and pull myself up into another realm. I used all of the metaphysical teachings I had ever learned. They became my lifeline, my silver cord connected to the Divine, pulling me out of the hole, dragging me out of the pit of fear and self-hatred. I was beginning to make my ascent out of the darkness and into the light. The Mrs. America Pageant became my way out.

When it was time for the announcement, I didn't know whether my husband wanted me to win or lose. My children were five and nine and, while they missed me because of the traveling I had been doing, I knew they thought it was pretty neat that I had entered and got this far.

And then came the announcement! I made the top ten. Then I made the last five. And then I was named third runner-up.

I felt some letdown. I had hoped I would win—every entrant there did! But I hadn't done badly. I'd become Mrs. California and had come in ahead of all but a handful of women from across the country. I suspect that my husband breathed a sigh of relief. He must have thought the shooting match was over.

If he did, he was mistaken. But then, who could have known I would become Mrs. Pancake of America?

• • •

This little slice of life had a point to it. Through it I learned what they were trying to teach me at my little church in La Crescenta. I learned the secret of prosperity.

All this while I had thought that prosperity was receiving. Now I knew that it was giving. Giving of oneself. Sharing of oneself. Participating.

My participation in the Mrs. America contest brought me to the attention of the Aunt Jemima people, since in the cooking event I had created a new pancake recipe that interested them. They asked me to become Mrs. Pancake of America! I quickly agreed and went on the road, traveling to twenty-six major cities in nine weeks, doing television (I had a ball on "What's My Line?"), and discovering that I loved this life! I loved doing television! I loved being interviewed! I loved the glamor and the attention and the excitement of it all!

As I began to travel and gain a sense of freedom, I knew that I could never return to the life-style I had before. I realized I would suffocate and die under that system. I felt guilty, of course. I felt that I didn't have the *right* to be this excited, this glamorous, and this attended to. I was the one who always paid attention to others.

I began to sense the adventure that was possible, the adventure of *life*. I did it! I was Mrs. California and third runner-up in Mrs. America! And I did it myself! I had no help from anyone. I did it on sheer determination, enthusiasm, and faith! My dishes were in the sink, but I was *alive*! There was a great feeling of power over my own destiny.

• • •

I went back to my church and my community and I gave, gave, gave. I gave of my talent and my time, and I noticed that what I received back was always a *greater* experience of life and a *greater* experience of myself, which I later realized was really a greater experience of my Self.

Finally, I began to get into giving money. I had never had money, so I thought, Give what you want to receive. It was hard at first, and it was scary.

I also began contributing to life in a way that made it possible for people to pay me for what I did. I began to realize that I was worth being paid. I had begun teaching a class entitled "Positive Thinking for Women Only," and now I began to charge for it. It wasn't much—ten dollars a person for four weeks. But I began to earn money on my own on a *regular* basis and never had to ask my husband for money when I wanted some small pleasure. I began to have independent buying power.

Later, when I was able to step back from my experience and see all of life contained in it, I realized that the feelings I was having were not exclusive to women. Many men also felt trapped in the same system at that time, a system that did not allow them to buy something for themselves that they really wanted because of what it would do to the family budget, a system that would not allow them to quit a job they hated, forcing them to continue working at something they disliked because, after all, they had a wife and children to support . . .

I knew that the only way out of that system for a man or a woman was to recognize their worthiness. We are *not* born in sin. This does not have to be our lot in life. We have a right to contribute whatever we want and be who we are!

I was discovering that the more I gave of myself in the ways I have been describing, the more I received. The more money I tithed, the more I received. The more energy I put into something, the more energized I felt coming out of it. The more time I devoted to a project, the more time it seemed I had for other projects that excited me.

This, then, *was* the secret of prosperity—and the secret of *life*. Life is for giving . . . and for receiving. We receive through what we give.

When I give, and only when I give, I can expand and express myself on all levels of my being, using all of my gift. This is what I learned in the Sixties and Seventies and what I continue to rediscover every day.

In our search we eventually discover that only through what we give to others, and never through what others give to us, can we define and declare who we are. Yet too many people look to what others give them—in the way of acknowledgment, in the way of glory, in the way of admiration and respect and salary and title and position—as the definition of who they are.

The wonderful part about the process of true self definition is that, while sometimes it looks as though we have no control over what we receive, *we always can control what we give.* Therefore who we are and who we become is always *ours to decide.*

Taking the First Step Means Making the First Move

Giving and receiving is the first step on the Inner Path. The exercises and affirmations given in the appendix are designed to help you take this step. Give all of yourself everywhere. Give the world your highest expression of Self. Do not worry about how you will survive if you do this. Rather, worry about how you will survive if you do not.

This was my deepest concern during the period following my discovery of Self, thanks to the teachings of a small church in La Crescenta. That discovery led to my being *okay* about expressing myself, which led to my putting together a little two-person traveling song-and-dance act for women's clubs, which led to my finding out about the Mrs. America contest and a series of events that sent me traveling around the country, appearing on radio and television, being interviewed for the newspapers, and having the greatest time of my life.

• • •

I knew when I came back to Pasadena that I could never disappear back into my old life again. I could never live another minute without being my highest self. I wanted more out of life than just adventure. I wanted a feeling of contribution. I wanted to know that what I gave meant something. In short, I wanted *to make a difference.*

That's when I decided to move into the ministry. There were, I knew, thousands of people just like me who had never lived their lives before, who had allowed themselves to be trapped in a prison of their own devising, who did not think it was possible to make any kind of contribution to life or experience, who were ignorant of any kind of expression of Self beyond the limited expressions they now permitted themselves.

There were, I knew, thousands of people saying, as I had once said, "There must be—there *has to be*—more to life than this!"

I wanted to speak to those people. I wanted to free them. This, I knew then, was my calling. It may have sounded presumptuous to the few friends I dared tell of my dream, but if dreams cannot be presumptuous, what is the use of having them? Do we really want our dreams restricted to ordinary things?

I began taking classes in Science of Mind at my little church in La Crescenta, then went to ministry school in Los Angeles, an easy drive from our home near Pasadena, so that I could be ordained in the Church of Religious Science. My husband was not sure what was going on with me . . . and I am not altogether certain that I was.

Finally I was ordained. But I still had a husband and a family. Surely, my husband ventured, I had no intention of taking a full-time job as a minister . . . did I? It was what I dearly wanted, of course. But he had a point. There were, after all, other things I had to do. Can one be both a good mother and a good minister to a flock?

I thought about that and came up with another question. Why *not*? One can be a *father* and a minister!

That's different, my mind argued. That's his job. Your job is to be a wife and mother, to hold down the fort, to keep the home fires burning and all that.

But what if I don't *want* to do all that any more?

Too bad, my mind declared. You settled for it; you have to stick with it.

I don't believe that, I argued back. A woman can be a

minister and do a fine job raising her children and be a wonderful wife, too, just as a man can do all these things and be a wonderful husband.

In the end, I compromised. I took a part-time position as an assistant minister in a small church nearby.

Then, of course, it happened. I got to loving, really loving, what I did. And the world—as the world always will when you are giving your best gift—wanted more of it. Word reached the Church of Religious Science headquarters in Los Angeles that I was enthusiastic, eager—and effective. I received a call to take over as full-time minister and pastor of a tiny congregation in La Jolla, California. A handful of people—about fifty, they said—had lost their minister and needed someone to lead their flock. Would I be the one?

My heart jumped just as it had upon my hearing about the Mrs. America contest. I had the exact same feeling inside. I shouted with joy, "Hey, *I* could do that!" I knew this was it.

I said yes.

• • •

For a while I tried to commute, spending time in La Jolla with my church family and time in La Cañada, about two and a half hours drive away, with my family at home. That did not work. I was required to be on call twenty-four hours a day to meet the needs of my congregation. I had to be there for the sick and the dying; I had to be there for the hurt and the frustrated. I had to be there not just for a few hours on Sunday morning, but all week long. I had a flock now, as well as a family. My chosen profession required more of me than a commuter could give. I asked my husband about moving to La Jolla. Perhaps he could commute to his job in Los Angeles. Many people did it each day by Amtrak. After all, his job, while an important one with responsibility, did not require him to be physically available at virtually any hour of the day or night.

Mistake.

Was I actually saying now that *my job was more important than his?*

Well no, not more important, really, just a little more demanding in terms of time, that's all—*potentially* a little more demanding, that is. One never could know when one would have to be somewhere, whereas in his job . . .

Mistake.

"*Your* job, the job you said you were *going* to do when you got married, demands only one thing: that you be *here*, in this house. That should be easy enough, shouldn't it?"

"Yes, but now I also have this job, and it requires me to . . ."

Mistake.

This was not an argument or a discussion I had with my husband; this was the battle I had with myself. And I could see that my dream was not going to materialize unless I was willing to give up a dream I had had once before.

I had to make a choice.

12. Step Two on the Inner Path: Forgiveness

Judge not, and ye shall not be judged;
condemn not, and ye shall not be condemned;
forgive, and ye shall be forgiven.

Luke 6:37

One of the hardest things to do in life is change dreams in midstream. This is because somehow, somewhere we got it into our heads that change is failure. It is extremely fortunate that these two words are not actually synonymous, because life is nothing *but* change.

In 1977 I made what until then was the biggest decision of my life. No sooner did I do so than I learned about the second step on the Inner Path. I found that after taking the first step—giving all of the real me I had to give and opening myself to receiving what the universe returned to me—I had a great deal of forgiving to do.

The person I had to forgive, of course, was myself.

Deep in my heart I knew I had done nothing wrong, and yet that was not easy to accept. After all, I had made the decision to leave my husband and children behind to travel to a new city and undertake a new career, which I thought myself almost unworthy of in the first place.

To put this in the starkest terms, here I was going off to be a minister, and the first thing I was doing to make it work was disrupting a home and family.

That was how I judged myself; that was the indictment. Once again, the prosecution and the defense waged their battle in my mind. The defense argued strenuously that for years I had given up what I wanted to do—given myself up, really—in order to meet the expectations and needs of others. I had a right to seek my own highest experience of Self.

But the prosecution always seemed to win. The gavel rapped. I was guilty.

For months I operated with this guilt. Through the years I have found that many people operate with hidden emotions, feelings, stirrings, and grumblings inside of them. They go through their daily lives ignoring these feelings as much as possible, and some become adept enough to do it for a lifetime. Others choose not to live with that inner turmoil over an extended period and face their quiet truths in a healthy, helpful way. Still others neither successfully override nor dig out these hidden feelings, these truths. They simply boil and simmer and then one day erupt in an unexpected and massive explosion.

I knew enough about the danger of this latter scenario to decide that it was not for me. I also knew I could not go on pretending to feel wonderful about my life on the outside while feeling guilty about my life on the inside. If I was going to be a minister, I had to live the truth as well as teach it. This I knew and this was my challenge. I also realized that I had no idea how to forgive myself. It was not a life skill I had developed. It is very hard to forgive yourself when you haven't learned how to forgive others . . .

As a child, I never could figure out why to forgive anybody. I never could figure out the *why* of forgiveness.

In church and in Sunday School I was always told that forgiving others was the Christian thing to do, but I never was given a reason to forgive other than that. Often, that just did not seem reason enough.

The truth was, my anger sometimes felt good, and staying

angry often felt even better. I can think of many cases in point, but there is one that I remember particularly well, probably because it was the first time in my life that I encountered the feeling that I really *should* forgive somebody. I was six years old and I didn't *want* to forgive that person, so I was very confused.

The episode involved my Grampa George.

Grampa George was my best pal. He was the man who loved me. He was my buddy. He was the man who let me follow him around, and if he had a hammer and nails, I'd get to have a hammer and nails, too. When he painted the shed, I got to paint, too. We'd march into the house together, both of us paint-speckled head to toe, and he'd announce to Nanny, "Well, we got that shed finished."

We got the shed finished!

I lived for a time in a house without men or boys, so when I went to live at the resort, it was wonderful to have Grampa George. I can still remember how he smelled—like kerosene and linseed oil. And he had sawdust all over him all the time. And he always wore bib overalls.

He protected me from my great grandmother whenever she wanted to spank me, and I protected him from her. When she wanted Grampa George and couldn't find him, she'd always send me. If I found him and he was doing something he wasn't supposed to be doing, I wouldn't tell on him. If he was at the local bar having a beer with his pals, he'd say, "Don't tell your grandma where you found me," and I'd say, "Okay."

• • •

I had been back with my Mom nearly a year and a half when she came into my bedroom one day with a strange expression on her face. She said nothing at first, just looked at me. I knew immediately something was wrong. And she knew that I knew. She patted the bed gently. "Terry," she said softly, "come over here," and smoothed out a place on the bed with her hands.

"What's the matter, Mom?" I asked, edging closer.

"Terry, something terrible has happened. Something just terrible. Your Grampa George is dead."

I heard her words, but they meant nothing to me. How could they? Great grampas don't die. Great grandmas maybe. On the porch, sometimes. Calling to children who won't come, perhaps. But great grampas? How could *they* die? They bang nails and paint sheds and get sawdust all over themselves. They don't *die*!

"Terry?"

It was my mother, back in the real world. Or was it the make-believe world? I couldn't tell anymore.

"Terry, listen to me. Your Grampa George is dead. I'm so sorry this had to happen . . . but you have to listen to me. There was an accident . . ."

Nanny and George were in their car in front of the resort, just getting ready to head off for a nice dinner in town, when a huge truck came along. As it approached, its driver took his eyes off the road for an instant to reach down for something on the floorboard.

The truck hit the car.

Head on.

Full speed.

I cried, of course. For hours. Nothing my mother could say could make it better. And for days I was furious. But I couldn't tell anyone about it. I knew what they'd think of me. I wasn't furious with the truck driver, you see. I was furious with Nanny.

Why couldn't she die and Grampa George live?

Why did *she* have to survive and Grampa George have to *die*?

My aching heart asked the question over and over again.

At some level I must have realized how unfair it was to be angry with Nanny for living, but I didn't care. If only one got to live and I had to choose, I would have chosen *him*.

It was a six-year-old's anger. It was an anger based on hurts and feelings with which no six-year-old should have to cope

but often must. And it was the first time in my life that I can
remember having to forgive. I needed to forgive Nanny. I
wanted to love her because she was, in her own way, wonderful, but I couldn't love her until I forgave her and so I needed to
forgive her. I needed to know that things didn't happen the
way they happened because of some personal choice she had
made. God didn't say, "Okay, one of you is going to die. Who
is it going to be?" Nanny always got her way, you know.

I needed to forgive Nanny and I couldn't, because I didn't
know what I needed to know, and there was no one to help me
discover it, because I didn't dare tell anyone how I really was
feeling. Had I been able to, I would have got back to the love,
because forgiveness is the path back to love. I didn't take that
path back for years.

Most important, I did not understand that forgiving Nanny
would not help Nanny, who didn't even know I was mad at her.
It would help *me*.

I didn't find this out until almost seventeen years later.

The Reason to Forgive

It was in my little church in La Crescenta that I made the
discovery of my life about forgiveness, and only as I began my
own ministry in La Jolla did I begin to remember it.

Not long after I began attending the La Crescenta church,
the minister announced that he was taking up a special topic for
a three-week series of lessons. "That topic," he said, "is
forgiveness."

Here we go again, I thought. To err is human, to forgive
divine. Christ died for our sins; the least we can do is forgive
others. Ho-hum.

I'd heard it all before and didn't need to hear it again. I liked
the little church, though, and didn't want to miss almost a
month of services just because I thought I'd be bored with the
sermons.

"Now a lot of you folks might think today's lesson on

forgiveness will be a little boring," the minister began the following week. "If so, I ask you to forgive me." The congregation chuckled. "Forgive me not for being boring, but for telling you you're wrong. There's nothing boring about one of the most powerful tools for self-improvement and self-realization ever discovered."

Hmmm, I thought, he's a good preacher. He can grab your interest. I wonder if he can hold it.

"There's more to this business of forgiveness than just 'making God happy' or being a good person," the minister continued. "The real reason to forgive is because it heals *ourselves*. To judge and to condemn others hurts you. Why? *Because the mind is a magnet.* It is the most powerful tool for creation in the universe. *Whatever you contemplate and give your attention to is what is going to come back to you."*

I felt as though I'd been hit by a lightning bolt. For the first time in my life, forgiveness made sense. *Practical* sense, not just spiritual sense. I later discovered that *all things that make spiritual sense make practical sense*, which is what I mean when I say that the greatest secret of life is that what appears to be the most impractical is really the most practical. "Seek ye first the kingdom of heaven and all else will be added unto you"; "Ask and ye shall receive"; "If a person slaps you on the right cheek, turn and offer him your left."

I drove home from church thinking about how much of my life I had spent judging others—and how much of the time I experienced others judging me. Which came first? I wondered.

I decided to pay more attention to forgiveness as a practical tool in my life. Then, like a lot of people with good intentions, I went back to my day-to-day existence and forgot all the lessons of the sermon.

• • •

And then there I was in La Jolla, and *I* had to give the sermon. How could I do that unless I believed it, lived it?

I knew it was no use practicing on myself what I was

planning to preach. I was going to have to practice first with someone else. I looked around to see who, besides myself, I thought I had to forgive, and I found the perfect subject.

My husband.

He was the perfect choice because it did not take me very long to realize he had never done anything wrong, so I had nothing to forgive him for, which was exactly what I needed to learn about myself.

My move to La Jolla was an effort to break out on my own, and my separation from husband and family was a very daring move for me. Never had I allowed myself to be completely responsible for my own life before, and now I was taking responsibility for the spiritual lives of *an entire congregation*— never mind that it had only fifty members. It might as well *already* have had five thousand! (Later on, when it did, I awoke some mornings unable to believe I was still its minister, much less that I had created that growth.)

My daughter Suzanne was graduating high school in just a few weeks and Rebecca was in the eighth grade, with only a few months of school left; it was not the right time for either of them to relocate, so they stayed with their father when I moved.

A few months later Rebecca did come to La Jolla, where she lived with me and went to high school. Susan continued on to college, and we never lived together again, although we have been with each other in the same city. She later relocated in San Diego so that we could be closer together.

For the moment, however, I was completely alone. My marriage was coming to an end. I had decided to begin a career of my own, and I had chosen the ministry as my calling. It was in that time of aloneness that I came to the realization that in order to teach the message I chose to teach I had to *become* it. That's when I really began to work with forgiving. That's when I began knowing that it was myself I needed to forgive. But I realized, too, that I didn't know how to do that. And that's when I began turning outward, to see if extending forgiveness to others might not be the answer. If I could find a way to forgive others, I might be able to find a way to forgive myself, I reasoned.

The one thing those early sermons in La Crescenta did provide me was a method. I could see the reason to forgive, all right, but very often I could not find a way to get past my own sense of hurt and frustration enough actually to let go and forgive the other person.

Now it was time for me to find a way. What I did not know, could not have known at the time, was that in finding a way to forgive, I was also finding my way along the Inner Path.

I decided to start with forgiving my first husband, because I recognized that I harbored many petty grievances against him. Even at first glance I had to acknowledge that most of them did not deserve even a moment's attention. Still, I didn't seem to be able to let them go. When it came to my husband, I somehow had a need to *make him wrong*.

Even though the children's father and I were not together, I was still talking with him a great deal, usually on the telephone and usually about the girls. He reflected back to me what were actually the same old self-judgments I was secretly convinced of—that I was a bad mother, a bad wife, a failure, couldn't handle anything responsibly, wasn't "doing it right." In these conversations, I performed mental gymnastics until I was absolutely haywire trying to prove to my husband that I was all right!

One day as I was talking to him and feeling this need to prove myself all right, I noticed that the reason I had called him was to ask him to do something for the children he had said he would do but had not yet done. All at once I had to laugh at myself. Here I was, pleading the case about my own okayness with a person before whom I was allowing myself to feel inadequate, inferior, and wrong, when *he* was the person I felt to be acting irresponsibly!

In that same moment I also became aware that he thought *I* was the irresponsible one and that he wanted only to handle his responsibilities to the girls in a way that he felt was right. Suddenly I began to see our situation multidimensionally, from both points of view, instead of unidimensionally, from mine alone. That changed my reaction to it totally.

I began to experience how, from his point of view, he could feel he was right. I didn't have to *agree* with his point of view, only *see* it, in order to experience this. I began to love him for the person he was and share with him that I knew he was doing the best he could in every moment and that I thought he was a wonderful father for doing this—for always doing his best. I began to find the good things; I began to find the value. I began to find what I loved, because he is a wonderful man, a beautiful being, and because of our mutual creation I have these beautiful children.

I began to see that in my earlier dealings with him I had been building my own case for resentment so that I could feed off it. And make no mistake about it, we do feed off resentment. It is an energy source.

Now, if you are going to do this, at least enjoy it. There is nothing wrong with this—it is just an experience. It is an experience you choose to have, presumably because you get something out of it. There is a payoff in it somewhere for you, and the payoff is what you are going for. So go for it and enjoy it! But when you decide one day that the payoff is no longer there for you, that your life is not sunshine and lollipops, notice how you have limited yourself.

Without love and forgiveness, you can never move into the unlimited joy and peace that you so desperately desire. *It cannot come to you any other way.*

• • •

I sat down and wrote my husband a note in which I told him all that I was thinking. I never felt so good in my life.

I rediscovered an old lesson in this. I saw once again that *everyone is "right" and everyone acts correctly from his or her own point of view.* Forgiveness is therefore not even the issue, but rather, *understanding another's point of view.* The end of disharmony can come more easily even than that—simply from understanding that there *is* another point of view.

Carl Rogers, the internationally known psychologist, author, and founder of the Center for Studies of the Person in La Jolla, has undertaken a worldwide peace project based on this thought.

Each of us is always doing what we think is right—even criminals will tell you that at some level they felt what they did was right when they did it or they wouldn't have done it. Each of us has a reason for doing what we do, and that reason justifies the action, making it right to do. What is actually needed is not forgiveness, but *an understanding of how the "error" could have been made*, in order that a change can be introduced.

This is how God sees things.

Forgiveness—of self and others—is the first step toward this larger comprehension. It allows us to let go of the pain and hurt that we imagine ourselves to have sustained through "unforgiveable" acts and thus to form a new and more comprehensive view of them.

Forgiving One's Parents

A good place to start practicing the use of this life tool called forgiveness is with one's parents. Most of us harbor some resentment against our parents, although we may be reluctant to admit that. This is because the parent-child relationship is so intense, and extends over a period covering so many crises and important moments. It would be a saint of a parent, indeed, who could negotiate all those interactions with his or her child or children without making a single error, or at least what their offspring might judge as error.

A number of things had occurred in my life for which I thought I had to forgive my dad. During a four-year period from the time I was three until I was seven, my parents were divorced, and I especially resented my father for that. They remarried and then stayed together until I was twenty-three, but I still allowed myself to move into my adult years angry with my father. Later, I couldn't let go of that anger. I remember thinking, If I forgive my dad now, I will have to deal with him; I'll have to bring him back into my life.

One of the great ironies of life is how we use pain to protect ourselves from pain, judgment to protect ourselves from judgment, and loss to protect ourselves from loss.

I finally did forgive my father once I realized that he'd done nothing wrong from his point of view and I had nothing to forgive. This realization came to me with the opening of my mind and heart to the truth I just stated. My father was just my father, and I was just me. Each of us was doing exactly what we had to do to move perfectly along our individual paths to Perfection itself. This understanding came to me through allowing my father to be exactly as he was all those years and recognizing that any upset I felt was the result of *my* laying blame on him for whatever I felt *I was lacking*.

I did not actually forgive my father. Rather, I allowed myself *actively to realize and consciously to experience* the truth that there was nothing to forgive and to *behave accordingly*. When I did, I found that we could talk, we could laugh, we could enjoy each other's company. Neither of us owed the other anything. We could relate to each other in a new and wonderful way—and I could love him, really love him. Today I adore this magnificent God-being, and I am grateful for the gift he gave me—my life.

• • •

In life, each experience we encounter can become an opportunity to love ourselves and others. You can be sure that such opportunities will keep coming up—your soul will keep bringing them up—until you have learned to love even your negativity. This is part of your process of life.

I started moving to love because I knew that I wanted to move to my higher vibration, I wanted to be the Christ-self that I knew I could be. (I will go into more detail about vibration in Chapter 14, when we talk about the greatest mystery of all, the nature of the soul itself.)

The End of the Arguing and Fear

I had decided at this point in my life that I wanted to become the highest and best me that I could imagine. I could see that all that kept getting in my way was fear.

The Christ vibration is the end of the arguing, and it is the end of the fearing and it is the end of the sitting over a glass of wine with whomever, and crying in your beer (which is a real miracle when you're drinking wine!) about how awful life is.

What replaced the arguing and the fear and the wallowing in self pity?

I don't know how it is for everyone else, but for me, when I became a minister I listened. I got people's feelings and their experiences, and I understood. I also allowed people to have the feelings and the experience they were having, telling them neither that they shouldn't feel that way nor that I was upset with them for having those feelings. What I got clear about is that their truths were not mine. Their truths were *their* truths.

We spend our lives trying to convince the other person of our truth. And you can't do that, because each one of us perceives the universe from our own viewpoint and *each one of us is right*. If I allow you your point of view, I can include you in my awareness and I am increased because of you and your truth.

The Highest Level of Forgiveness

In order for me to begin using forgiveness as an effective tool in my life I had to know that I was one with God, the master of my own life, the creator of my own destiny, that everything in my life I did because I wanted to. Nothing ever *went* wrong, I did what I did because I wanted to.

Understanding this feeling of being one with God and therefore totally in charge of everything that happens to one goes far to explain Jesus' forgiveness of all those around him. The hardest thing for people to grasp, the thing they have had to grapple with and have found so difficult to emulate, is Jesus' incredible level of forgiveness. Even in the midst of his being nailed to the cross, even in the midst of his dying, he was able to say, "Father, forgive them, for they know not what they do."

This is the highest level of forgiveness. We cannot understand it, much less duplicate it, unless we have a Christ Consciousness, which allows us to see *the perfection in all of life*. Only a Christ could see *his own part in all of it*. The only reason Jesus could do what he did and say what he said is that he knew the truth. He knew that he wasn't being hurt, that he *couldn't* be hurt. He knew he wouldn't die, because he came here on purpose to remove a curse from humanity. The curse was the curse of the vengeful God in which all of mankind believed. I have come to know this through my own experiences in the world; I have come to this remembrance through my own inner seeking.

As I went through the big transition in my life, I was confronted by criticism from the press because I was what they called a "prosperity minister." I kept getting the kind of coverage that made me out to be some kind of sex- and money-hungry evangelical con artist.

What I began to understand was that everyone to whom I spoke had their own truth. In every interview I gave, that other person had his or her own perceptions, and for them what they saw was true. What they saw and what they felt was *their* truth. In many cases I had an entirely different truth, and that's just the way it was.

I began to realize that I either could try to get people to love me so that *I* finally could love myself, doing whatever it took to get everyone to say, "Isn't Terry Cole-Whittaker wonderful?" Or else I could start to love myself, allowing others their truths, and not trying to convince them of my value or get their approval.

I chose the latter. I chose to love myself, live my vision, be true to my truth, become my own ideal, and love everyone else so that anyone in my presence, if they chose to, would *fall in love with themselves* out of my totally allowing them to be who they are and accepting them without condition.

This, to me, is what forgiveness is. Forgiveness is refusing to judge, refusing to love in any way except without condition. This, to me, is a major step toward heaven, a major step toward God. And this was a step I wanted to take as I began my ministry in Southern California in 1977.

I didn't know it when I started, but I still would be taking this step eight years later as my ministry ended.

• • •

It was early June 1985, and it had been a busy day, with the telephone ringing constantly and people moving in and out of my office in whirlwinds of excitement or worry, depending upon their task. They were excited if it had to do with our new Foundation for Spiritual Study, the search for other, more modest quarters, or locating facilities for our new seminars and workshops. If it had to do with money, they were worried.

Our debt was considerable and every day brought a letter or a call or a personal visit from vendors with whom we had done business, some of them polite, some not so polite, all of them worried about whether they would be paid now that the ministry was no more. We established a formal, scheduled payback plan and communicated our commitment to each of our creditors in writing. Most received this news with a sense of professional, businesslike appreciation for the professional, businesslike way we were going about the task of repayment, knowing that we could just as easily have declared bankruptcy and released ourselves from any pressures and obligations. A

few apparently thought this was not enough and felt the need
to add even more pressure.

I had to forgive them if I was to get through my days. I had
to seek to understand their point of view. I had to do the same
with some of my former employees, many of whom now
apparently felt the need to attack me. Some were granting
media interviews in which they described me and the ministry
in terms that had not been true for them two weeks earlier.

The days were filled with incidents requiring me to "put up
or shut up" on the issue of forgiveness, just as others were
required to do the same with me. It was during this period,
toward the end of spring and the beginning of summer 1985,
that I saw more clearly than ever that taking Step Two on the
Inner Path was not a one-time thing. Neither, for that matter,
is taking Step One. You have to give everything you've got to
give *in every moment* if you want to make your next moment
the highest there is. And you have to forgive—or, to use a
more accurate term, allow—life's experiences for the same
reason that God allows them: in order to provide you with
more and more opportunities to grow.

Since the process of growing never stops, Step Two on the
Inner Path is necessary. So it was that at the conclusion of my
ministry I found myself taking the same steps I was taking at
the beginning.

Our office space was daily being stripped of its furnishings
and accoutrements, with everything we no longer needed sold
off or given to charitable organizations. We wouldn't need
much. Terry Cole-Whittaker Ministries had taken up the
entire top floor—over 11,000 square feet—of the building we
were in. The Foundation for Spiritual Study would require less
than one-tenth that space. Our old staff of over forty employees plus the volunteers who manned the mailroom, phone
banks, our publications office, and other areas produced a
throng of seldom less than seventy people bustling about. Now
fewer than a dozen could be found.

We wanted to pay off our ministry debt as rapidly as

possible, and did so partly through the sale of our typewriters, computers, desks, and chairs. With the disappearance of these furnishings the place looked more deserted by the hour. Suddenly, the office seemed cavernous. The enormous space acquired an almost surrealistic quality, with overhead lights on here, off there, a swivel chair with a desktop calendar on its seat standing alone in the middle of a huge room.

There was a sense of something dying, of something very useful and very empowering suddenly disappearing. I was the one who had caused the disappearance and sometimes, as I wandered through the barren space gazing at a stray picture on the wall or a still-connected telephone on the floor ringing away with no one to answer, I was not sure myself why I did it or how it happened.

I imagined this feeling to be what many people experience in the wake of major, life-changing decisions. It was melancholy mixed with euphoria mixed with second guesses mixed with regret mixed with elation. One minute I was up; the next minute I was down.

Had I done the right thing?

Of course I'd done the right thing.

Was my work in the ministry over?

Without question it was over.

Did I really wish to move on now to a new adventure?

I *had* to move on now to a new adventure.

• • •

The phone on my desk rang. It was an old friend inviting me to take a break and step out for lunch. "Great idea!" I told her. "Meet me in front in ten minutes."

I hung up, smiling. Life was wonderful. No matter how things looked in the moment, life was wonderful. Everything depended on how one chose to hold the experience of "now." I started out of my office, heading for the reception area.

"You can't go down that way!"

It was one of my staff people, catching up to me from behind.

"They're down there right now!"

"Who, for heaven's sake?" I asked.

"The TV people. They've been standing there for two hours with a microphone and camera, waiting for you to come out."

I laughed. News crews had been after me for an interview for weeks, ever since my final church service. Their maneuvering had begun to seem like a contest to see who could get to me first. The crews camped outside of my house at six o'clock in the morning, and they were there when I got home at night. I simply brushed past them with a wave and a smile and a very sweet "Hi, guys. No comment," every day. Now they apparently were going to stake out the office.

"Why not just go down and give them an interview and get it over with?" I said. "They'll follow me all the way to the restaurant otherwise."

"No, *no*," my associate advised. "You can't! They're out to crucify you!"

"Oh, I don't think so," I disagreed. "They just want a little footage on me, that's all. Then they can satisfy their editors. I'm going to go down and talk to them."

"Don't!" my associate warned. "You'll be down there for hours. And they're going to ask you about your financial problems. I heard it from one of the volunteers who overheard them talking to each other when she came in. Terry, they're just trying to make you look bad. Why give them the chance?"

I hesitated.

"Just this time, go down the back stairs," she continued. "You can get in and out, and they'll never see you. You don't need more bad publicity right now."

"No. I'm going out the front way, and I'm going to tell them I have a luncheon date and that I've got appointments all afternoon but that I'll give them an interview tomorrow."

My colleague rolled her eyes in exasperation.

The news crew approached me as soon as I appeared.

"Uh . . . I'm Mike L., ma'am, Channel __ news?" the one in the snappy red sport coat offered tentatively. "This is my technician, Steve S." (I am fictionalizing the identity of both of the people and the station here.)

"Hello, Mike." I shook hands. "Hello, Steve. Aren't you the same two who were across the street from my house this morning before dawn?"

"Yup," the camerman nodded, looking a bit worn.

"Well, I can't stop just now, but I'll be glad to give you an interview tomorrow."

Mike's eyes brightened. "You will?" he asked. Then, regaining his newsman cool, "How about this afternoon?"

I shook my head briefly left to right. "Can't. Calendar's full. It'll have to be tomorrow." I could see what they were thinking. "I won't talk to anyone else between now and then. You have got the exclusive," I said. "You've earned it."

• • •

When they arrived the next day I gave them two hours of my time. It was supposed to be a short interview, but Mike seemed like a nice person. He was a young man, and he told me this was his first big assignment. He thanked me four times before the interview began for "giving me this break." He was so grateful, I found it easy to keep talking to him as long as the camera kept rolling. When we were through I realized I had given him enough footage for a full-length documentary! Mike knew it, too.

"Gee, thanks for all the time you gave me," he said genuinely. "The people in the newsroom aren't going to believe it when I walk in with this. I don't know how they're going to use it. They weren't expecting this much. Hell, they weren't expecting anything."

I liked Mike, and I had a sense that he liked me. We seemed on good terms, especially for people from two different worlds.

I turned to my colleague as Mike and Steve left and mentioned this. It did nothing to erase the worried expression from her face.

• • •

It was 2:30 the next afternoon when a former congregation member and most devoted volunteer, whom I shall call Betty, came into the office, her voice filled with concern.

"I drove in as fast as I could. Is Terry okay?"

Everybody gave her a blank stare.

"Hasn't anyone seen the midday news?" Betty asked.

Nobody had. "We don't watch television around here in the middle of the day," someone explained.

"Well, didn't anybody call? Haven't you heard?"

No one in the office had heard.

I overheard the exchange outside my office.

"Betty? Is anything the matter?"

She whirled in surprise. "Terry! I didn't know you were in there!" She moved toward me. "Terry, you have got to call the station and get them to run a retraction."

"Why? What have they said?"

"It was all over the news. They were practically accusing you of embezzlement. This Mike person was showing pictures of financial statements and check stubs on the screen—someone from this office must have given him those—then he would intercut this with comments you gave to him. When did you give this guy an interview?"

"He was here yesterday for over two hours," my colleague interjected as she walked up to us.

"Well, he did a nice hatchet job on Terry," Betty told her. Then, turning to me, "You should sue the station. At the very least, you have to demand equal time."

I put an arm around Betty's shoulder and walked her to my office. "Oh, I'm not going to go on television, Betty, and I'm not going to sue anyone."

"But, Terry, they've made you look so bad! They're trying to make you look like an irresponsible, flighty lady who started a ministry then—"

"Betty, that doesn't bother me any more," I interrupted. "I don't care what they say about me."

"But . . . but," she stammered, "it makes *us* look bad."

"Us?" I asked. "You mean the ministry? Betty, there is no more ministry. Haven't you seen them taking the furniture out of here? And all the equipment? The ministry can't be hurt, Betty, because the ministry no longer exists."

She moved away from me then, pacing the room for a moment, looking at the walls and out the window as if trying to find cue cards somewhere that would tell her how to say what she wanted to say next.

"I'm not talking about the ministry, Terry," she finally said. "I'm talking about those of us who have supported you. We've been sticking our necks out supporting you all these years, and a lot of our friends and relatives have made fun of us, actually laughed at us." She spoke the words sadly. "Well, I guess they'll really have the last laugh now."

Now I understood. If I didn't defend myself and people believed whatever it was the station was saying about me, *she* would look bad.

"Betty, I'm so sorry if anything I have done has damaged you," I said softly, going to her. "I always have been grateful for the assistance you have given us, and I know it took courage to stand up and be counted in a way that made a difference."

She looked at me, and I thought she might cry.

"It's the end, isn't it?" she said. "This really is the end."

"Yes, Betty, this is the end. I no longer have a need to do what I had been doing in the ministry. Nor do I have a need to justify myself in someone else's eyes. People will form whatever judgments they want to, anyway."

We walked to the door together, said a few more words, embraced, and then she was gone. My colleague came in moments later. "You gave that reporter the interview of his life," she said, "and he used it to try to hang you."

I said nothing.

"Aren't you even a little upset? I can remember a time when this was the kind of bad news we used to say we had to 'keep away from Terry.' You befriended that reporter yesterday and he betrayed you. I would have a hard time forgiving that."

"There's nothing to forgive. I don't feel damaged in any way . . . although I think Betty does. I am the same person, made of the same stuff, doing the same thing I was before I knew about this. Nothing has changed in my life in the last fifteen minutes that would make me want to choose upset over peace, anger over joy."

I walked back to my desk. *And you're right*, I said to her silently in my thoughts. *This is a little different from what it was for me before. I am not the same person that I was then. Thank God.* "Thanks for your concern," I told my associate. "I love you."

I relate this incident because it is a good illustration of how one can react to life when one consciously travels the Inner Path and actively seeks to take Step Two every step of the way.

In the old days I would have been hurt by what that reporter had done. *I trusted him*, I would have said to myself, *and look what he did to me.*

I would have been hurt by Betty, too. But this was a new time and a new place, and everything seemed different now. How did I get here? I mused over the situation for a while, pondering all the things that had gone on in my life in the months most recently past. It was this reflection that pushed me farther along the path I am taking now.

Today, in my workshops and seminars, sponsored by the Foundation for Spiritual Study, this is what I share about forgiveness:

Not wanting or being able to forgive another creates a tremendous blockage to living your life to the fullest. Ask anyone who has held a grudge for a very long time. Anger kills. Hatred and resentment maim—in a very real sense, not just in a figurative sense. However, they kill and maim the people *from* whom, not *to* whom, they are projected.

It is the people with anger in their hearts who suffer, physically as well as mentally. Yet physical and mental health are not the primary reasons for moving to a space of forgiveness. There are much higher, much more compelling reasons than that.

Forgiveness is one of the tools through which you can empower your life to cause miracles to happen. The person you have to forgive is yourself.

There is only one problem with accepting forgiveness. In order to accept it for ourselves, we have to offer forgiveness to others. This is because we cannot fathom receiving something we cannot give.

Our whole society needs forgiving because our whole society is built on the concept that you "did something wrong." We are raised to think of ourselves as sinners, even if we cannot remember a single offense ever committed against another.

Preachers pontificate about our sinfulness from the pulpit, and teachers "remind" us of it from the lecturn of the Sunday School classroom, so that even small children know the story of Adam and Eve and original sin. Sooner or later we all absorb the message. We were *born* in sin. We have sin in our souls.

If it isn't original sin we believe in, it's "karma." Either way, we've done something wrong before we ever got here, and we're going to have to use this life to *repent and make up for it.*

What's interesting about this scenario is that some people accept these beliefs because they feel they have to, thinking such acceptance to be the only way to get to heaven. Others reject these beliefs altogether, calling the whole game, including heaven, ridiculous.

The good news is that sin is nonsense but heaven is not.

Heaven is the experience of the highest expression of Self,

and if you've had even the beginnings of such an experience only once in your life, you know what heaven is.

Forgiveness is the way back to God, not penance or anything you must do to "make it better." Forgive yourself for all offenses, real or imagined (later you will discover that they are all imagined), and use this as a tool to change the feeling you have about yourself so that you can love yourself again. Forgive others you imagine to have offended you, so that you can change your feeling about them and love them again, too. By this simple act of *grace* is love reborn.

The terrible irony of most people's understanding of God is that, precisely because they think God is vengeful, they are vengeful, too. And it is precisely because they so often *don't* forgive that the pain and loss associated with human relationships—person to person, group to group, or nation to nation—continues. Only forgiveness can end the cycle, only forgiveness can turn the tide, only forgiveness can set the stage for a new script to be played out.

Shakespeare had it right when he said, "All the world's a stage, and all the men and women merely players." What he could have added is that they are also the playwrights. Unfortunately, without realizing it, the scripts they are writing often turn out to be tragedies. If their human dramas produced happy endings, we would then see that the system—the usual source of guidelines for writing scripts—works.

But it does not.

Too often, it fails.

And so, we continue to seek a better way, a new world. But the new world is not to be found outside ourselves, it lies within. That is the secret. The same is true of the path it takes to get there.

Forgiveness is a major issue along that inner path. That is why I have taken the time to deal with it here. (In the appendix are some exercises and affirmations to read and use as practical, hands-on tools in dealing with forgiveness right now.)

• • •

I left the office shortly after my discussions about the television interview, having found that I wanted a change of energy. It was a beautiful June day, and I meant to keep it that way. There would be no more hurt, no more fear, no more anger in the life I chose to lead. I walked away from the office and, in a sense, although I spent many more hours and many more days there over the next three months, I never returned again. I never went back to where I was in the days when that office and everything it represented had been the most important thing in life to me.

I turned my back on my old life for good.

13. Step Three on the Inner Path: Guiltlessness

And the land be subdued before the Lord:
then afterward ye shall return,
and be guiltless before the Lord,
and before Israel; and this land
shall be your possession before the Lord

Numbers 32:22

The summer of 1985 went by quickly. By its end I felt as though I were in a new place in a new time, a stranger in a strange land. Nothing was the same as it had been twenty-four, eighteen, or even twelve months earlier. The frustrations were over. The ministry was officially dissolved and the Foundation for Spiritual Study was formally operating as the new and much smaller entity under which I chose to do my work. I was living for a temporary period on the island of Maui, following through on my promise to myself to spend at least six months in Hawaii resting, rejuvenating, and recharging.

The only actual work I did was to facilitate a series of week-long retreat seminars sponsored by the Foundation and to finish this book. At another point in my life, what I had done in the past year and a half, what I was now doing, and the decisions I was now making for the future would have triggered massive attacks of guilt. In September of 1985 I felt no guilt at all.

Not that I didn't have some temptations. When I let some key staff people go in March and April, among them some who had been very close to me, I did not have an easy time of it. I didn't want to hurt anyone, but I had to keep going. My role in the ministry was over for me—it has been for quite some time—and I hoped that my friends would understand.

I also had an opportunity to feel guilty during the summer, when I was sued by a former contract vendor.

Finally, there was the fact that when I dissolved my organization it was in debt.

This last problem, in particular, occupied my thoughts as I moved into the second half of 1985. No one likes to be in debt. No one likes to owe another. Yet I could not allow myself to fall into the trap of guilt. Guilt paralyzes, guilt numbs the creative sensitivities, guilt absorbs every last bit of energy and drains the Self of desire, motivation, and control. I'd had enough of that in my life, but the summer of 1985 was a new time for me and I was experiencing life in a new way. And so I felt no guilt at all.

• • •

At one of our small retreats on the island near the end of the summer, the question of guilt—and how I was able *not* to feel guilty—came up.

"How do you do it?" someone asked me.

"How do I do what?" I asked back.

"Keep pushing forward and keep smiling no matter how many mistakes you've made."

"I've never made any mistakes," I deadpanned. The group laughed uproariously. "I'm serious!" I insisted. The group laughed some more.

When the laughter died down (and by this time I was laughing with them), I smiled at my questioner. "What I've discovered," I said, "is that everything I have done, and everything you have done, and everything that has ever been done by anybody, has been perfect. There are no mistakes, and there is no such thing as error in the cosmos. I have also discovered that we *think* of many things as mistakes. We judge ourselves many times as having been wrong, and forgiving ourselves is a lot more difficult than forgiving another."

"Tell me about it. I know," my questioner interjected wryly.

I said, "There's only one way I can do it, and that is by getting in touch with, by aligning with my concept of God."

Someone from the side of the room chimed in, "But it feels like we're talking about more than God here. We're also talking about right and wrong and our entire system of value judgments."

"That's right!" I agreed. "And to me it's all wrapped up in the same thing. How I feel about myself and my God deter- mines how I feel about myself and life, myself and my actions, myself and what I call right and wrong—all of it."

"How *do* you feel about yourself and right and wrong?" I was asked.

"I can forgive myself anything and have already forgiven myself everything."

I looked around the room.

"Now, that may sound arrogant, and yet I can't retract the statement even to get your approval, because the statement is true for me. My truth may not be your truth—it doesn't have to be. But I have found a key, a way to make a quantum leap in my spiritual evolution, and I see it as the logical third step on the Inner Path. That key, that way, is what I call guiltlessness.

"Guiltlessness is the realization that I have done no wrong at any time in my life, and neither have you. We are now living, always have lived, in a state of innocence and perfection."

I could see that, even for my seminar participants (or some of them, at least), this was a bit far out.

"I don't know," one of them mused. "That sounds a lot like we're just letting ourselves off the hook."

"We *are*!" I concurred. "Why shouldn't we? God does."

"Who says so?" a woman in the group wanted to know.

"God says so," I told her. "And if you don't want to listen to

God, listen to Supreme Logic. Supreme Logic says this: *Nothing happens in the universe that God does not allow.* If something is allowed by God, then it cannot be wrong. Only those things not allowed can be wrong. Yet *if a thing is not allowed by God, how can it happen?*"

Silence.

Then, from the back of the room, "God may allow something to happen, but that doesn't mean he *wants* it to happen."

I said, "I am not sure I understand. How can anything occur that God does not want to occur?"

"Easy. God gave human beings free will; God gave us the ability to do as we wish."

"Yes, that is correct," I said, "but how is that the same as saying you can do something God does not want? Is it not more logical to assume that you can do whatever you wish, and that *whatever you want is what God wants*? That eliminates contradictions, no?"

"But how could God want me to do all the dumb, stupid things I have done? Or, for that matter, all the incredible, horrible stuff that mankind has done?"

"If God did not, how could they have happened? Do you really see God as this impotent being sitting around somewhere saying, 'Oh my gosh, it's happened again! Oh, I wish they would stop that!' Is that how you see God?"

"No, I don't see God as a person. I see God, or what we call God, as a force, an energy, a fact of the universe."

"And this force or energy, do you think it has a mind of its own and therefore a personality of its own?"

"No, I don't see it that way."

"How do you see it?"

"It is simply there. It is just What Is. It is a unifying concept or principle. It is an energy, as I said—a force."

"Without intelligence or thought?"

My friend stumbled. "I don't know. That doesn't sound right. It sounds more right to say that the force *is* intelligence.

It is pure intelligence, without adulteration, without subjectivity, without judgment. That's what it feels like to me."

"Great. I now have a better idea of your concept of this thing we call God. But let me ask you something. Does this force or energy or pure intelligence do anything? Or does it just kind of lie there, inert?"

"It . . . it doesn't do anything; it *is* everything. Do you understand?"

"Yes." I smiled. "Yes, I do. But do you? Do you hear what you yourself have just said? If it is everything, then it is *everything*, not just the good things or what you *call* the good things. It is *every* thing. It is you, it is me, it is the atom bomb, it is Hitler, it is Mother Theresa, it is every one and every thing. Correct?"

A long pause.

"I don't know. I think so, yes, but I haven't thought about it at that level. I have to say, I really haven't. So maybe I have to say, I don't know."

"That's okay. Not knowing is the highest state of being. Only when you do not know are you open to the impossible. When you think you know, that is when you start deciding what is possible."

"Interesting as it is," a man sitting on the floor to my left interjected, "what does this discussion have to do with 'right' and 'wrong'? How does this relate to your statement that you've never made a mistake?"

"It has everything to do with it," I replied, "because Man reacts to the universe in the way that he conceives it. We experience life in the way that we *understand it to be*."

The room was quiet.

"Now if God is *God*," I went on, "meaning that which is all powerful, all knowing, all creating, then nothing can happen against his will unless he *chooses* it to happen against his will, in which case it would not be against his will at all.

"If God is a force, an energy without specific personality but

with supreme power—that is, the All and the Everything—
then all things that are *are God.*

"In either hypothesis, and any other you can propose, *there
can be no polarity;* there can be no 'right' and 'wrong.' There
can only be that which God creates or that which God is.
Nothing that is can be outside of God if God is all that is, and
nothing that is created can be created by someone or something
other than God if God creates everything.

"So we confront the ultimate dichotomy. In a world of
polarity—fat and thin, tall and short, up and down, left and
right, good and bad—we find there is nothing but unity. All
things are the same thing. There is only one thing and we are
calling it by different names."

We broke for lunch then, but the discussion went on over
our meal and into the afternoon session of our seminar, as well
it might. After all, the same discussion has been going on since
time and life began. The subject of guilt versus innocence has
been haunting theologians and religionists for centuries. Not
many years ago someone could have been hanged or burned
for saying what has just been said here. The hangings and the
burnings would have been conducted in the name of God by
those who through the years came up with rationales for a
thunderous, vengeful God of wrath. Since they believed in a
God of wrath, they felt justified in acting like one. Yet theirs
were the statements that did not square with many people's
deepest intuitive feelings of the truth, which prompted the
discussions in the first place.

People who have the courage, the wisdom, the openness, and
the faith to undertake a deep, personal examination of the
issues I have raised here are the people who will change the
world, just as they have been the world changers throughout
history. And that's what we're talking about here—changing
yourself and changing the world.

"Mistakes" Are Lessons,
So Get Rid of Guilt

God is love that knows no condition. That is what I told the courageous and earnest searchers and seekers who came to our seminar, and that is what I am telling you here. The truth is that God cannot be damaged or destroyed and therefore has no reason to want to *get even* with those of us who have done things that we ourselves call wrong.

God allows us to grow and experience who we are—that is our purpose in life. God has nothing to forgive. He—the Force, the Energy—simply *is.* The Bible answers the question of who or what God is. *"I am that I am."*

If you did not allow your child to play with matches, but he played with them anyway, finally one day nearly setting a fire, you might be tempted to think you had cause for punishing the child.

On the other hand, suppose that you gave your child the matches deliberately, so that he might have the experience of them and decide for himself how and when to use them. And supposing you did nothing more then but *watch over your child every moment* to make sure he didn't burn himself but only learned about matches?

Likewise does your Heavenly Father watch over you, and the good news is that you will not burn, neither in the everlasting fires of hell (which does not exist), nor anywhere else.

Look, then, upon your most grievous misdeeds as lessons, learning opportunities, and get rid of guilt.

That's just a recommendation, of course. That's just my good idea. If it serves you to feel guilty, for goodness sake feel it. Feel guilty and experience what it does to you—to your body, your creativity, your energy, and your happiness. If you want to feel guilty, then *feel* it. Get into it and roll around in it. The only reason to have a feeling is to enjoy it. There are people who do enjoy guilt, you know. Immensely. If you are not among them, or if you are tired of guilt and the energy drain that it is, dump it!

If I'm going to have any feeling associated with guilt, it's going to be guiltlessness. Being guiltless will take you back into innocence, back into a space of childlike wonder, excitement, and purity. It will open you up to greater creativity because the attack on yourself has been terminated and you are free to express yourself. *You* are guiltless. None of what you have done is wrong in the highest sense. There is no such thing as wrong in God's world, and there is, therefore, no one who will judge you.

• • •

Guilt is a common experience and this planet is riddled with it. When I'm into the drama of my life, I can feel guilty about everything—and at one time I did. I felt guilty if someone in the room was unhappy. When I was a young housewife giving dinner parties, I felt guilty if the conversation stopped. Whenever my husband was simply moody, I would feel guilty. I would ask myself, What did *I* do wrong? What should I do to make it better? At times I thought that if I hadn't been born maybe others wouldn't feel so bad or have it so bad. I'd think, if I just got rid of myself, these people—parents, husbands, kids—wouldn't have all these burdens, all these problems. If I'm causing pain in these people's lives, they would be better off without me.

In those days I was also angry. Guilt and anger go hand in hand.

If you believe in guilt, you believe in punishment. You believe you need to pay a price. That would not be surprising, given the race consciousness of the planet. Others may have told you that you owe them. Society has definitely told you what you owe the world.

If you are a joyous, happy being, you often are called foolish in our society. You are considered a flake, a real nut. How can you be totally joyous when the world is falling apart? (This is a question I was asked all the time when I was a minister.)

To be guiltless and happy is to risk being called selfish and uncaring. The thing to do is keep walking. Walk away from guilt and a belief in punishment and condemnation, and walk toward guiltlessness and the knowledge that God is love. The Bible says that thousands will fall on your right and thousands on your left, and this will happen. People in your life will suddenly look at you differently. They will fall away, in the sense that they will no longer choose to be close to you because they can't play the guilt game with you any longer. Just keep walking.

It could even be your family that falls away. Because your family feels one way is no reason you must feel the same way. Your environment, your background, has nothing to do with it. The behaviorists say it has everything to do with it, but it has *nothing* to do with it. Evolutionists will tell you their story, yet *we* are the creators who have evolved life to this point. *We create evolution.* We are not the product of it, but the creators of it, and we have become greater through it.

If you feel guilty about something, anything, look to the very source of it, seek to discover its cause. Do not be the product of your past. Be the creation of your present moment in the experience of joy.

I know this may not be easy.

Sex and Guilt: The Great Connection

Where does our guilt come from? How does it start? Part of it is associated with our experience of sex. This is neither surprising nor unimportant, because sexual energy is the life-force energy, one of the most basic and powerful energies we experience.

I felt guilty about my sexuality at a very early age. I could sense in the adults around me feelings and thoughts centered around sex. Human beings pick up feelings, especially children and those who remain childlike. A child does not have to understand words to know what is going on. Even today you often know what is happening with people around you before you hear them speak.

We live in a sea of emotional vibrations. That's how a child knows candy is good before she ever tastes it. She looks around the room and picks up the vibration when the first person says, "Oh, let's give the baby some CANDY!" She hears the feeling of joy!

As a child I was very aware of the emotional vibrations emanating from sexual energy, not only in my family but among my family's friends, on television, in the movies, in novels, in society in general. Among the messages I received from all these were: Don't touch yourself; don't show yourself; there is something wrong with your body; there's even something vaguely wrong with going to the bathroom.

I heard adults joke about sex, hide their words from me. Before long, I began to feel that my body had "okay" parts and "nasty" parts and that I had "okay" feelings and "nasty" feelings.

The religion of our society is sex. It is the underlying energy that moves most people. That is why I am discussing it here. Why does sex have such a powerful influence? Because the purpose of copulation is reproduction, the continuance of the species. In order to have a body in which to come back to earth, you must have a man and a woman join together in this singular act and allow you to become their child. We have taken this beautiful tool of creation and have built an entire society around it. And somewhere along the line we have become ashamed of it. Even reading about it in this passage may be uncomfortable to some.

It was this same sort of discomfort I sensed as a child. It wasn't that anyone was communicating these things to me verbally. They didn't have to. I felt their repression, I felt their frustration, I felt their desires, I felt their guilt.

What I was feeling, of course, were their memories. Those vibrations I mentioned earlier are actual physical sensations, not conceptual frameworks or nonexistent imaginings. Thought vibrates. If you don't think it does, talk to any pathologist, criminologist, or psychologist. We have long since learned that we can measure the energy of the brain, the energy of thought. The soul remembers everything. What I was feeling in the vibrations of the persons around me as a child were my inner memories of sex.

The soul remembers not just the physical sensation of sex. The entire history of the sexual activity of humankind is within the soul of each person. Hence, I could feel the fear in women that they would lose their man to another woman through sex. I could feel the intense sexual desire and lust within men and women.

Our society has deteriorated and turned a simple, loving act of reproduction into an obsession for a physical feeling. There is so much pain, expectation, and attachment to sex that it literally controls the lives of many people.

Religion has controlled people through sex; governments rule on sex. We are constantly being told what we can and cannot do with this most precious and most personal possession called our sexuality.

We feel guilt deep within the fabric of our energy vibration because of our race's sexual past. We remember it and are not allowed to forget it. As a woman I have felt much pain and fear because of the sexual abuse of women and children throughout history. I could not forget it if I wanted to. My great grandmother was terrified that I would someday be molested. When I was four or five, she used to read to me from the newspaper about little girls who had not watched out and then been sexually abused.

I don't think my story is so unusual.

It is the guilt about sex that produces all the abuse. People are dying because they have repressed their vital energies. People are raped and attacked because of guilt.

The only release from this guilt is through forgiveness, self-love, and knowing yourself as spirit. In my own awakening I went through many steps and processes to restore myself to self-love and sovereignty. I know that who I am is beyond a body.

This is the thought that saves. It saves all of us from guilt and brings us into the experience of guiltlessness. Only from this perspective can we see the perfection of all things, the unity of all things, the innocence of life itself. As long as we think of ourselves as only a body, we cannot gain perspective, because we experience life only as the body experiences it, which is how we got into trouble to begin with.

How Guilt Can Run Us

I first began to think about dropping guilt as one of my main emotional experiences when I started going to a metaphysical church occasionally at the age of seventeen. But I was so caught up in the philosophy that "this world is it" instead of "I'm it" that my awakening was very gradual. By the time I was twenty-three and going to my little church in La Crescenta, I had begun to read more and attend services regularly. I started feeling better about myself. Still, I was far from being free of guilt. And the thing about which I felt the most guilt was just wanting to be *me*.

It is ridiculous that we are born into this life and then feel guilty about being here, expressing ourselves, being happy, and living as we choose!

When I first started my work in the ministry in La Jolla with that tiny congregation of fifty people, I knew that I wanted to make a difference in the world. I knew I wanted to be well known and successful. I even knew that I was a performer, an entertainer, and a teacher all wrapped up in one. I am a multidimensional being—we all are—and I wanted to express all of me! There was only one problem: guilt about doing what

I wanted to do. You see, the way a minister was expected to be and the way I wanted to be were two vastly different things.

A minister, according to tradition and the preconceived notions of the public, was supposed to wear robes, be and act conservative, and make everybody happy by becoming whatever it was the congregation expected you to become. This did not necessarily include being who you are, especially if that included being a television star!

My conflict was great. The battle raged within me. Should I try to fit the minister ideal or be my own ideal?

I used to wear my hair in a bun because that was a minister look, then let it down, flowing around my shoulders when I was my real self. I had my minister clothes and my real-self cloths. I didn't want to upset anyone by being or expressing my Self.

And all of this wasn't just what I imagined I had to do. There were members of the congregation who told me outright when I disappointed them. I now see that they were only disappointed in themselves, yet at the time I was always trying to please and always feeling angry, guilty, and martyred.

This is probably not much different from your own experience. You may not have been in the ministry (or you may have been), but chances are you have been in a position in which you felt specific things were expected of you and you were not allowed to be yourself (or didn't dare take the chance of finding out).

My life's major encounter with guilt actually began before I entered the ministry and arrived in La Jolla. It occurred during the time I have already described, when I first knew that I really wanted to express myself in different ways and emerge from the cocoon in which I had been living—around the time of my involvement with the Mrs. America contest.

In those days the average woman projected all her needs onto her husband, who was supposed to be her Answer and her Everything. Meanwhile, the poor man had to go out and battle the world (in his mind) and be *his own* Answer and Every-thing, all the while thinking that his wife was *his* answer. Then he'd find out she wasn't so he started with someone on the side . . . and then the wife would start to think about having someone on the side, but being a woman, that's another story.

I came face to face with the ancient dilemma of all male-female relationships, and my process of creating a loving and equal partnership of God-beings began. Four divorces later, I have that.

• • •

I know my experience may not sound like the best example to follow, but I pursued the only direction I could find at the time. This book is intended to save you some of the steps along the path that I have taken. That is not to say I took any wrong steps. For me, they were all exactly what I needed to experience in order to be who and what and where I am today. Today I see the perfection in it all.

But back then, though I knew it was time for me to live my life, I felt massive guilt, mixed with incredible fear.

It was at that time that the women's work force started to grow; women were just beginning to trickle into the power structure of society. I was one of those in the vanguard. People who are in the vanguard of things often feel guilty. There's this vague sense of doing something one is not supposed to be doing. In the case of women working, that was definitely true. Most wives did not have jobs, unless they "had to work" to help put food on the table or had inherited a business—or unless they were teachers. Teachers were always okay. Being a teacher was all right somehow.

So when I first started to do things on my own, I'd often have horrible feelings in the pit of my stomach. I remember feeling negligent and really suffering inside if the house was untidy or if the children were sad or had an unhappy experience. I'd think, Oh-oh, I should have been here. I could have prevented it.

Since that time I've come to realize that children grow up and do exactly as they choose, and the biggest error one can make is to feel responsible for every minute in the lives of one's offspring, which is not at all the same as being responsible for providing a loving, safe, nurturing, and empowering home life.

Once again, I'm sharing these details of my life with you not so that I can tell you my story, but simply as a means of illustrating how the move to guiltlessness goes, sometimes inch by inch, step by step.

Eventually I broke out of the guilt I was feeling, and I did so by practicing some of the principles I was learning at my church.

The people at La Crescenta were saying, "Your life is your own. You can have it any way you want it." I finally realized that if I kept feeling guilty about who I was and what I was doing, I would have my children thinking that I *should* be guilty. Others pick up on our feelings and then take them for a ride!

To stop feeling guilty I used affirmations. I affirmed, "My children are happy, joyful, healthy, and loving beings." I would say to myself, "When I work, it empowers my children to be responsible."

It was time for me to stop trying to make everyone feel good and to begin to live my own life. Little by little I did this. Little by little I felt better and better. And little by little my children took on more responsibility for their own lives and their own feelings.

The issue of guilt had to do not just with my children, of course. It had to do with my husband, my family, my friends, and neighbors—with everyone I feared was judging me.

We all get into this maze. The way out is to stop playing Wonder Person and to begin to tell the truth about who you are and what you want. That is what I had to do, and I could begin only once I finally realized, "It is now or never. In some lifetime I am going to have to wake up, and in some lifetime I am going to have to heal myself."

This is what happened to me.

But even when I got to La Jolla and my own pulpit, I still hadn't "arrived." I was still making my way along the Inner Path and had yet to find guiltlessness; I hadn't yet taken the third step.

All of us are traveling the Inner Path. Some of us make it complicated for ourselves so we can be sure to get the lesson and the wisdom. I was going in the direction of God, the light, and freedom in a roundabout fashion. And yet all I was looking for is all anyone is ever looking for: more love and more life. Exchange the words *love* and *life* with the word *God* and you will find they are all the same thing.

All of us are looking for love. If we don't get love from one person, we go out and get it from another. Then we feel guilty for wanting more love and finding it. All of us are looking for more in life. If we don't like the job we have, we start looking for another. Then we feel guilty. If we don't like the house we've built, the clothes we bought, or the car we drive, we feel guilty. We're programmed to think we should be satisfied with what we have, with our lot in life.

Did anyone ever tell you that you made your bed and now you have to lie in it? Did you believe them?

The problem is that we mentally sign contracts and make agreements that commit us for the rest of our life, but have no way of knowing what we are going to be faced with or do *tomorrow*! Yet to break any agreement wreaks havoc in our lives because then we are breaking our word, which is supposed to be sacred. I've come to realize that the only sacred agreement I can make is to be me, ever unfolding.

I began to see that the very systems I had created for my own security became my own prison. This is something we all realize sooner or later.

The La Jolla Church of Religious Science began flourishing soon after my arrival. There was continual growth. I was pleased with how things were going, yet I was plagued with the fear that it would all fall apart. I felt guilty when I was playing because I felt I should be working—my work seemed like play to me! I felt guilty about my success when others were struggling. I felt guilty about wanting to have my life my way. In short, like a "good person" brought up in the Judaeo-Christian ethic, I felt guilty about all that was joyful, fun, and pleasurable.

Guilt as a Means of Control

I was telling someone about this thing called guilt as I was writing this chapter, and he asked me an interesting question: "How do you know that some of the feelings you've had were not the Higher Self telling you that what you are doing or how you are being is not the way you want to act and be?"

I told him that guilt is never a calling from the Higher Self. The Higher Self never uses guilt to wake you up. We use guilt because we believe it serves us, and we will keep using it until it doesn't serve us any longer.

I used guilt to control myself and others. Now I know that I don't need a device to control myself, because I can be trusted to make the highest choice, to do the right thing by my definition (which is the only definition that counts). And I know that others do not need to be controlled, either, because they cannot hurt me or damage me in any way, and so I can trust them now, too. I harm no one by being myself and living as I choose.

Trustworthiness is the key that opens the door of guiltlessness. Learning to trust yourself and standing by your own decisions allow you to walk through that door. Acknowledge yourself and uplift yourself into greater glory. That is why you are here! And know that you can never use anyone, because everyone else is also doing what he or she believes will bring more glory.

Accept yourself as the cause of your life. To me, being the cause of my life puts it all on me. What I think and feel, I create. What I give out, I get back. It's that simple. If I want love, I give it, and when I give it, I am it.

As you walk the Inner Path, know who you are and what you want and always tell the truth about that. Keep on walking. Refuse to play the games of the world, for there is so much more in store for you than the illusory rewards they promise.

If you want to rid yourself of guilt, first examine who controls you with it, then notice how you use it to control others. And examine what you fear would happen if you released guilt.

In the appendix you will find some exercises and affirmations that I have used to help myself. With their help, I was able, whenever the desire came up in me to make someone else feel guilty or to make demands, to allow myself to have that desire, then let go of it. I would share with others what I wanted, but I would release them to be who they are and to do what they wanted.

· · ·

Do not confuse not being guilty with not being responsible. That is most important! Responsibility is a virtue, guilt is not. Responsibility is a form of self-love, guilt is a form of self-hate.

To be irresponsible is to run away. To be responsible and deal with life is to give yourself power. Some say I ran away because I stopped the ministry. What I actually did was make a courageous decision to bring to a close, to complete, what no longer gave me joy. Completion is not desertion; ending is not running. When you complete an experience in life with openness and honesty, that is not the same as running away. To run away is to believe that you can hide from yourself. Yet all of life is your mirror, which you discover when you run from anything.

Responsibility *is* a form of self-love, and ultimately we all see more value in self-love than in self-hate. Being responsible means being responsible to yourself first and foremost. A master is free of the world. Masters own themselves. You will come to realize that your Self is the most important thing there is. All there is is you, and you are the All and the Everything. When previously we talked about the All and the Everything, we were talking about *you*.

This is your opportunity now, today: to begin your great Adventure of the Soul. This is your opportunity to take the three steps you have been given, using the exercises at the end of this book to help you, and to venture where few people have ventured—into the realm of their own mastery.

Some people might say, "If I didn't think I'd feel guilty, I wouldn't show up tomorrow to do my job." Well, if you're showing up to do the job in order not to feel guilty, leave it. You are killing your Self.

If you catch yourself saying. "If it weren't for how guilty I'd feel, I would leave this relationship," leave it. If you are staying in the relationship in order not to feel guilty, it is killing you.

You do not have to die for others. You have the right to live for your Self.

14. The Purpose and Function of It All

> To every thing there is a season,
> and a time to every purpose under the heaven:
> A time to be born, and a time to die;
> a time to plant, and a time to pluck up
> that which is planted;
> A time to kill, and a time to heal;
> a time to break down, and a time to build up;
>
> A time to weep, and a time to laugh;
> a time to mourn, and a time to dance;
> A time to cast away stones, and a time to
> gather stones together;
> A time to embrace, and a time to
> refrain from embracing;
>
> A time to get, and a time to lose;
> A time to keep, and a time to cast away.

Ecclesiastes 3:1-6

> And we know that all things work together for good to them that love God,
> to them who are the called according to His purpose.

Romans 8:28

For centuries people have yearned to know the reason for their being, so it is not surprising that, of all the questions I have been asked through the years, the one that has come up more than any other is: "Terry, what is the purpose of life?"

And those who ask are usually surprised at my answer. "There is no reason for being," I tell them. "There is no

181

purpose *per se*. That doesn't mean that life has to be purpose-less. It simply means there is no *given* purpose."

Life has no purpose, because life is a force or energy that produces an experience. The experience it produces depends upon how the force or energy is used. *You* are a force or energy—what we might call pure spirit—and how you experience your Self depends upon how you use the spirit that is *you*.

Because life does not have a purpose per se, you are free to assign it one at will. (That is what is meant by free will, not the ability to do something God opposes. It is not possible to do something God opposes. You are the All and the Everything and you cannot oppose yourself.) In this, as in all things, your will is God's will and *Thy will be done on Earth as it is in Heaven*.

The fact that life has no inherent purpose does not mean life has no function. As you know, function and purpose are two different things. Function is *what* a thing *does*; purpose is *why* it does it.

The function of life is to feel. Life functions through feelings and produces more feelings as it functions. The *why* of the feelings is up to you. You can feel whatever you want, but *you cannot avoid feeling*. That is how life functions.

• • •

Now I am going to say some things about feelings and make some claims about life for which I have no proof. If you are looking for a book that gives you proof for each hypothesis, put this book down. I am producing this book entirely out of my personal experience. That may not be good enough for seekers of empirical data. Yet what I have discovered could change your life. It certainly has changed mine!

What I have come to realize is that feeling is the prize. Feeling is the human experience. Feeling is the power that creates. I have alluded to this before in this book, and now I would like to elaborate.

When I talk about feelings I am talking about something

very physical and very real—an electromagnetic force field, in fact. The force field is so strong that it sends up a vibration that pulls like vibrations to itself. *It is a magnet for similar energy particles.* The result: more of those situations that produced the feeling to begin with.

Now this may sound far out, but I encourage you not to dismiss it out of hand. Consider the following:

- Failure begets failure and success begets success, according to human behavior specialists who have reason to know.

- We have been exhorted in poem and song for years to "put on a happy face" and "whistle a happy tune."

- Psychologists and psychiatrists agree that a person's disposition is a key to his mental health.

- Medical doctors have likewise accepted for centuries that a patient's state of mind is half the battle both in maintaining good physical health and in achieving healing.

- As enlightenment has come, some doctors are now even suggesting that state of mind is the *whole* battle.

- Religionists have proclaimed from the very beginning that, given the proper state of mind, there *is* no battle!

What we see here is a consensus. A great many highly intelligent people with diverse backgrounds and vast experience have come to the conclusion that *how you feel about things* can be a determining factor in *the way you experience life.*

Think about it. Everything you do, you do for the feeling. Certain feelings have an attraction for you; certain feelings are repellant. All of your actions are designed either to achieve a certain feeling or to avoid one.

Do not underestimate the attraction even of feelings of pain . . . or guilt. The fact is that some of the most "negative" feelings hold attraction because they give us a heightened experience of our Selves that we think we can get no other way.

They prove to us that we are alive! Ask any daredevil why he does what he does, and that's exactly the answer he'll give you. He climbs that canyon face or jumps those cars on his motorcycle because of the *feeling* he gets when he does it. We call it danger; he calls it excitement.

Now I am going to repeat something I mentioned earlier, because this could well be one of the most important things I have to say in the book:

> *The more we experience any given*
> *feeling, the more we are going to*
> *experience it in the future.*

It is for all the reasons given above that history repeats itself. And history will stop repeating itself only when we grow tired of the feelings we get when it does and discard them.

Feelings and Forgiveness:
At Last It Makes Sense

Earlier we talked about forgiveness as an important step on the Inner Path. Now you are about to find out why, in the specific sense, forgiveness works.

Forgiveness is a virtue, we are told, but the truth is that *forgiveness is totally unnecessary.* It isn't needed. It is simply a path back to the feeling of unlimitedness, the feeling of love. We only seek forgiveness or offer forgiveness when we want to change the feeling we are having. It is a tool, nothing more and nothing less, to *change feelings.*

• • •

Feelings are more than the function of life, *they are life itself.* They are the soul.

People have been asking whether the soul exists and if it is immortal.

The soul exists.

The soul is immortal.

The soul is *feelings*, and it remembers every feeling it ever *was*.

The soul doesn't have feelings, it *is* feelings. Whatever feeling you have, that's what the soul is in that moment.

Have the feeling of love and the soul is love.

Have the feeling of fear and the soul is fear.

Because this is so, you actually define yourself by the feelings you have. By the feelings you have you choose who you are, and by the feelings you have you also create your reality.

Now, there are some who might think this unfair, but this would only be those who perceive feelings as something over which they have no control. If the way you feel about something, anything, is *totally* under your control, the proposition seems eminently fair, because it would give you a practical tool for affecting and improving the soul and thus affecting and improving your life.

In this discussion you have just been given the most powerful and practical secret of life:

> *Feelings are the holiest force*
> *in the universe (they are the only*
> *reason for life), and the feeling*
> *of love is the holiest of the holy.*

That's the powerful side of it. The practical side of it is

> *We can have any feeling we wish*
> *simply by being it.*

The interesting thing is that all this can often be accomplished with more ease than it can be discussed. It is one of the few things in life that may be *easier done than said*! Talking about "being a feeling" presents some interesting challenges. It is one thing to say "be happy," but the real question is, How do you do that? It is one thing to advise, "Be at peace," but by what means is this done?

The answer is part of the experiment in human experience and behavior we are conducting right now through the Foundation for Spiritual Study. It is an informal experiment, not a scientific research project with measurable results, control groups, and published reports of our findings. Still, it is an exciting undertaking which we think could be of real importance to humankind. (Our experiment is explained in more detail in the next chapter of this book.)

The answer to "how" lies in a concentrated effort to be totally conscious and totally aware. Focus your attention only on the feelings you wish to project and therefore have, and on the image you have created of the person-God-being you wish to be.

That sounds a great deal more complicated in theory than it becomes in practice. The formula can be more simply stated, *Be who you are.*

The only difficulty in translating that injunction into action is that many people do not remember who they are, or do not believe it.

We have been taught that this physical world is the full domain of the universe, and that if you can't see it, touch it, taste it, and smell it, it is not real. But this physical experience we are now having is but the tip of the iceberg. There is much more beneath the surface, much more unseen than is seen.

What we have done in our society is block our feelings, mainly because we are afraid of those that we judge as bad. If you put all of your energy into stopping the feelings that you judge bad, you are also stopping your *other* feelings. In your effort to prevent loss, you restrict your body, restrict your brain, lock in your soul, and place the entire entity in the fear vibration.

The trick is not to stop your feelings, but to control them.

The idea is not to repress them, but to select them.

A master is one who chooses the feeling he wants to have and has it. The highest master is one who always chooses love and joy.

You've just been given the secret of the mastery of life in one paragraph.

• • •

Feelings are energies, and all we do is go around matching them. Walk into any room and watch how everyone picks up the feeling of everyone else. It's almost like a contest—the strongest feeling wins. If Christ walked into the middle of a war zone, the vibration of his spirit would immediately lift everyone.

Feelings are our soul connection. They have nothing to do with the physical, with the body.

When you die, your spirit takes the soul information out of your body and you leave. You think the body has died, but it has done nothing of the sort. All that has happened is that *you have left*. The body keeps right on living *without you*. It simply changes form, because you are no longer there and no longer need it to exist in the form you required in order to be your perfect temple. So the body returns to clay, whence it came. You think you are not one with the earth? You *are* the earth, vibrating in a different form, moving at a different speed. You and the earth *are the same stuff*.

Scientists are every day making astonishing "discoveries" about life and the universe. I put the word *discoveries* in quotes because they are not discoveries at all, merely confirmations of what philosophers and theologians have been saying for centuries.

Recently, one scientist announced that according to his analysis the chemical and molecular structure of trees seemed remarkably similar to that of man. Indeed, he theorized that all of the objects of the universe may contain trace elements of the same common denominators. In other words, while objects are certainly different in many ways, it may well be that *no object is totally different from any other.*

• • •

The Great Adventure of the Soul awaits you. Decide that the purpose of life is to take that adventure. Follow this exciting experiment: Endeavor to have the happiest, most joyous, most loving feeling that you can create in every moment. If you do this and nothing more, *your entire life will change for the better within forty-eight hours.*

Remember what I said a few chapters back—that sometimes what seems the most impractical turns out to be the most practical? In the case of immediately and materially improving one's experience of day-to-day life, that is profoundly true.

Nothing could be more impractical than what I am doing now. Yet it is the most thrilling, exhilarating adventure I have ever been on. It had better be. It is for this that I gave up Terry Cole-Whittaker Ministries.

15. My New Direction: The Divine Experiment

Is it not written in your law, I said, Ye are gods?
John 10:34

I t is September 17, 1985. When I awoke early this morning there were twenty people in my house. Some were meditating, some were out watching the sunrise, some were in the kitchen quietly preparing breakfast. All are involved this day in the Divine Experiment.

As I walk to the front of the hideaway retreat site we have been leasing for six months on Maui I am embraced by a 180-degree, cineramic view of the ocean. Over my shoulder the Haleakala Crater rises as a backdrop to the scene in magnificent, awesome, 10,000-foot splendor. Rich, lush vegetation covers the earth, and a short walk away a pool of diamond-clear water invites me to wade in a basin formed by ancient volcanic rock, a swimming pool of the gods.

I am in paradise.

And I, too, am part of the Divine Experiment.

The experiment is this: to see how magnificent an expression of Self it is possible to achieve in *this moment*; to see how much love, how much joy, how much peace, how much happiness, how much fulfillment, how much excitement it is possible to experience *right here in the present.*

The experiment is this: to see how much awareness, how much wisdom, how much insight, how much understanding, how much patience, how much compassion, how much acceptance of self and others it is possible to share *immediately.*

The experiment is this: to see if it is possible to be and experience and share *all of it. This minute. This second.* In this fraction of life we mark by time and space and choose to call now.

The experiment, I am overjoyed to report, is proceeding well. It is succeeding.

The people who came to this island to be with us this week came because they felt they needed a place where they knew they would be loved, accepted, supported, and empowered to be their most magnificent Self. That is what the experiment is all about. There are very few places where it can be safely conducted.

But there will be more places soon.

I pad out to the hot tub—my bare feet feel good against the cool patio floor—and am startled again, as I have been every morning since coming to this paradise, by the freshness of the morning air. I want all air to be that way. Climbing into the tub, I glance over my shoulder and catch the end of the sunrise. It takes my breath away, and I want, in this moment, to experience all sunrises like that.

In the hot tub, I feel the water, the giver of life, warm me, caress me, wrap me in its swirls of bubbling, vibrant energy. I breathe deeply and relax into the experience. Waving to somebody in the distance, then hearing the murmur of voices from the kitchen, I reflect on what it is like to be here, right now. Nearly two dozen people are living together under the same roof, and I observe that no one is on anyone else's nerves. There is no pettiness, judgment, or criticism; everyone seems to be smiling all the time. And why not? Has the group not come together to acknowledge love?

I get out of the tub and walk over to the outdoor shower, smiling all the way. I love the sensations I am feeling. I love the feeling of being so happy to be alive and being alive to be so happy! The shower water hits me and I shriek a joyous shriek. The contrast of the cold of the shower with the warmth of the hot tub renders me instantly effervescent. I throw back my head and laugh, just laugh, at the ecstasy of it all.

At that moment, someone inside turns on the retreat center's sound system. A song called "Flash Dance" rides the morning air. At once my heart picks up its beat. The song's lyric line at just that point provides the perfect finishing touch to a perfect encounter with life. "What a feeling!" the singers sing, "I can have it all!"

Suddenly, I find my feet moving. I need more room. I leave the shower stall. And there I am, dancing on the patio. I dance and laugh and become as a little child, returning to the total abandonment that comes with just-being-there-being-happy.

And in that moment I want everyone in the world just to be there, wherever "there" is for them, and be happy.

In this moment I want everyone just to be there and be happy. That, to me, is what this book is all about. That is what my new life is all about. It is about the exhilaration and the excitement of the glory of each new day. It is about living in peace and harmony with everyone and everything around me, in total alignment with the universe and with a sense of oneness with every other being.

That is the experience open to everyone who is willing to embark on the Adventure of the Soul. That is the opportunity available to all who undertake the Divine Experiment. That is the destination of those who travel the Inner Path.

The chance that we all have is the chance of a lifetime to step out of the world as it is and to create the New World as we would have it be.

Once we looked for someone else to do all this for us. Many people thought world transformation would come from the top down. We looked to our world leaders. We looked to our religious figures. We looked to our poets and our philosophers and our songwriters and our novelists. We looked to them for years. But they were having none of it.

Then we started looking to ourselves. We began quite a while ago, quietly at first, so as not to attract too much attention, then with more and more daring, more and more openness, more and more insistence. One day our "leaders" looked over their shoulders and saw us. They read the signals. Loud and clear. And they started taking action. Slowly, of course. Reluctantly, to be sure. But they did take action.

They had to. They had no choice. We were leaving them in the dust.

And so it is that major alterations were made in the very fabric of our lives—in religion and in government, in business and in industry, in arts and entertainment, sports and leisure, science and technology.

So it is that the Roman Catholic mass may now be offered in a language everyone in the church can understand. So it is that women may now be Jewish rabbis and Anglican priests. So it is that songs are now made to end world hunger and films are now made to end world hatred. So it is that doctors and scientists now come together in the hope of preventing a life-ending world illness (which the newly combined effort in AIDS research hopes to do), and governments may now be brought together in the hopes of preventing a life-ending world conflict (which the Rogers Peace Project hopes to do).

These changes will continue over the years just ahead and will gain in impact and speed until the world is transformed and better suits our individual and collective consciousness. The building of the New World will not proceed from the top down, but from the bottom up—as all things that truly stand forever are built.

I am participating in the Divine Experiment twenty-four hours a day, seven days a week. It has become the focus of my life. It is the work to which the Foundation for Spiritual Study is dedicated. We are seeking the experience of spiritual, mental, emotional, and physical mastery. We are attempting to transcend our limits in all areas, to step beyond manmade laws and world opinion. We are seeking to establish a new world.

And we are not alone.

Communities are already forming and will continue to form all over America and throughout the world, some spontaneously, some by long-range advance design, wherever the principles of thought, word, and deed I have outlined here have become the basis for communication and interaction. These communities are being established by individuals who are waking up, who are tired of war, tired of crime, tired of judgment and attack, tired of poverty and illness and disease. They are being established by people who are using pure reasoning as the basis for their action.

Why would Life Eternal create a magnificent being on a beautiful and bountiful planet and then say, "You are condemned to sickness and struggle, after which you must die?"

Pure reasoning will tell you that this is insanity.

Pure reasoning will tell you to seek a better way.

This is what I am doing now. I am seeking a better way. Not for the world (which I saw myself doing as a minister), but for myself, for I have come to know and understand that if world transformation is to take place, it will take place in individual hearts, souls, and minds, ultimately resulting in a new collective Consciousness. We will all simply *be* a certain way, and our being will change the world, whose being will no longer suit us at all.

The programs of the Foundation excite me because they are wide open, not static; divergent, not clustered (no two people experimenting with us are doing it in quite the same way); safe, not dangerous (no one is criticized, laughed at, or excluded because of their beliefs); and expanding, not contracting (we seek more life, more love, more expression, more magnificence for everyone, knowing this is the only way we can have it for ourselves).

Our movement in the directions I have outlined takes many

forms and can be seen in the way we live our daily lives—in the way we eat (an entirely new nutritional program is being experimented with that could have dramatic effects on health and life), the way we sleep (we are looking at what goes on in our dreams and even seeing if there is a way we can program our mental activity in the dream state), even in the way we breathe (rebirthing and other deep breathing cleansing techniques have become standard, and valuable, tools).

In the Divine Experiment we are making bold and outrageous demands on ourselves, such as the demand that we be willing to use 100 percent of our brains instead of the usual 10 to 30 percent most of us have been operating on. We are also asking the unaskable questions—Can I live forever? Can I create what I dream and desire? Can I experience places beyond this physical realm?

One hundred years ago the idea of these things happening would have been ridiculed as preposterous. Today, with all that we know and all that we know we will know in just a few more years, it almost seems preposterous that they would *not* be happening.

Can there really be much question that as more and more is discovered about the power of the mind, more and more of what the mind can imagine will come into our reality? Do out-of-body experiences even now sound more commonplace than unusual? Is the New World of Tomorrow really so far away, or is it just around the corner?

There are those who say we can't have Utopia. My truth is different. I am experiencing more and more of what Utopia must be every day in my life, and I see no reason suddenly to be experiencing less. The experiment in which I am engaged is an attempt to see *how much more* I can experience, and I am already discovering there is no limit.

No limit! That is the key. That is the most accurate descriptive phrase. That is the truth. We are, all of us, limitless. We have come here, all of us, to experience our limitlessness.

As I said in the preface to this book, this is the most exciting period of my life. Things are happening for me that most people would never dream possible. I am having an experience of life that brings feelings to exalt the heart, open the mind, and stir the soul.

Feelings are the function of life. Feelings are the prize. How are you feeling about your life today? Would you like your feeling to be different? Better? Happier and more joyous?

Turn the page and go on to the next chapter.

16. Where To from Here for You?

"Come to the edge."
"We can't. We are afraid."
"Come to the edge."
"We can't! We will fall!"
"Come to the edge."
And they came.
And he pushed them.

And they flew.

Appollinaire

T his is it! This is going to be the most exciting part of the book! But don't get into this chapter unless you're in a daring mood, because this chapter is going to dare you! It's going to *double*-dare you! And the next chapter is going to challenge you even more. It is going to be unlike any other chapter of any other book you've ever read. That's because YOU ARE GOING TO WRITE IT.

Through the first fifteen chapters you have been exposed to *my* truth and *my* feelings. I am now asking you to co-author this book, because what is really important is *your* truth and *your* feelings.

• • •

What I am going to ask you to do right now, without putting this book down and coming back to it later, without thinking about it for a few days or talking it over with a friend, is take part with me in the Divine Experiment. This is an opportunity to discover who you really are and to create who you choose to be.

The rest of this chapter will be a questionnaire. It is designed to allow you to identify your feelings about yourself and your life. There is no score at the end of the questionnaire, and there are no correct or incorrect answers. This is simply a device to bring your feelings to your own attention.

Chapter 17, which follows, is yours to write. You will copy the questions and write the answers on separate sheets of paper or in a notebook. I will give you a little help along the way. Although it will be separate from the book, it will be part of the book, and it will be the most interesting chapter of the book so far, because it will be about the center of your universe and the being around whom all life revolves, *you*. It will deal with your life and how that has been, as well as how you now wish it to be. When you are through writing it, you will see that you have done more than engage in a solitary exercise. The chapter you will have written will have a profound impact on you and every person whose life touches yours.

This is it! This is the time you have been waiting for. All these years you have been asking for a sign, a signal that the time has come to make your move. *This is the sign.*

Sooner or later you have to decide—where to from here? Sooner or later you have to choose where you want to go with the rest of your life and how you want it to be when you get there. *Now is your chance to do that.*

You can turn this book from a passive to an active experience in the next two minutes. You can make this book not just *info*rmational, but *trans*formational.

It's up to you, just as your whole life is up to you.

Pick up a pen and take out a notebook or some paper right now. On the paper, answer questions 1 through 76 in the questionnaire below. Do not list the numbers ahead of time, as some of the answers require more space than others and you will not know how much space to leave. Simply begin by answering the questions one at a time.

Questionnaire

1. I understand that this is an inquiry designed to allow me to reveal my feelings to myself about a wide variety of subjects, many of them personal. I am

_____ (a) happy to be answering this questionnaire

_____ (b) feeling unclear about its worth but not sure I want to abandon it

_____ (c) certain that answering these questions is not something I want to do and therefore unwilling to go on

2. My life right now is

_____ (a) marvelous

_____ (b) okay

_____ (c) horrible

_____ (d) not really horrible but not really okay, either— somewhere in between okay and horrible

3. My present financial situation is satisfactory and while, like all of us, I would like to do better, I have no real complaints. TRUE or FALSE

4. The last time I saw my parents was _____. This is

_____ (a) okay with me

_____ (b) not okay with me

5. I am living in a home that I would most accurately describe as

_____ (a) magnificent

_____ (b) marvelous and more than I need

_____ (c) okay and accommodating of my needs

_____ (d) okay but less than I need

_____ (e) a real hole-in-the-wall

6. I am so enthusiastic about my job that some days I can't wait to go to work.
   TRUE or FALSE

7. Right now, if I had _____ more dollars, all my problems would be solved.

8. I don't have any present problems related to money and so the above question does not apply to me.
   TRUE or FALSE

9. Of the things that bring human beings happiness, the most important to me is _____
_____

10. If I could live the last three years over again, the one thing I did that I would change would be _____
_____

11. I would change nothing I have done in the last three years.
    TRUE or FALSE

12. I have the perfect relationship right now with a significant other and am happier than I have ever been where relationships are concerned.
    TRUE or FALSE

13. I hope no one ever sees the answers to this questionnaire, because if they do I could be in trouble.
    TRUE or FALSE

14. On a scale of 1 to 10, I would rate my life right now a _____.

15. On a scale of 1 to 10, I would rate my car right now a _____.

16. Sex is not important to me, and it is okay if I go weeks without a sexual experience.
    TRUE or FALSE

17. My partner is more interested in sex than I am. _____
    I am more interested in sex than my partner is. _____
    I am okay with the above. _____
    I am not okay with the above. _____

18. My income each month
    _____ (a) matches my needs
    _____ (b) exceeds my needs
    _____ (c) does not meet my needs

19. If I feel resentment toward anyone or anything in my life, it would be toward _____ because:
_____
_____
_____

20. My present thought about God and religion is that
_____
_____

21. When I get on a scale or see myself naked in a mirror I say:
    _____ (a) "How nice it is to be my perfect weight!"
    _____ (b) "I've got to, *got to*, stop eating all that junk!"
    _____ (c) "Good grief! I'm going to disappear! I had better start eating more."

21. If I were to rate how I feel about my wardrobe, I would say:
    _____ (a) I am ecstatic.
    _____ (b) I am pleased with it.
    _____ (c) I am not pleased with it.
    _____ (d) I am frustrated and sometimes angry about it.

22. If I were to rate how I feel about my sex life, I would select the following answer from above: _____

23. I am in the career field that is just right for me and I see no changes needed or desired.
    TRUE or FALSE

24. If I could change anything about my career right now, it would be
_____ (a) the money
_____ (b) the title and other perks
_____ (c) the amount of recognition I receive
_____ (d) the actual work I am doing
_____ (e) nothing at all
_____ (f) something not listed here, namely: _____

25. If I could know that money would not be a problem, I would quit my job tomorrow.
TRUE or FALSE

26. If I did not think I would be hurting another or would feel guilty for the rest of my life, I would leave my relationship right now.
TRUE or FALSE

27. If my mate left me tomorrow, I would be
(Select as many as apply)
_____ (a) shocked
_____ (b) amused
_____ (c) amazed
_____ (d) dismayed
_____ (e) angry
_____ (f) hurt
_____ (g) relieved
_____ (h) afraid
_____ (i) delighted
_____ (j) grateful
_____ (k) devastated
_____ (l) peaceful
_____ (m) not surprised
_____ (n) unhappy

28. The last time I laughed so hard that I cried was _____ days/weeks/months/years ago.

29. From the time of my first sexual experience until now, I have never had a better lover than I have now.
   TRUE or FALSE

30. While it is difficult to reduce life to such simplistic terms, the three most important things in life to me from the list below are:
   _____ (a) financial security
   _____ (b) spiritual clarity
   _____ (c) job satisfaction
   _____ (d) marriage or relationship
   _____ (e) acknowledgment
   _____ (f) sexual companionship
   _____ (g) family ties
   _____ (h) health
   _____ (i) feeling fulfilled
   _____ (j) life purpose

31. The *five* most important would be: ___, ___, ___, ___, ___.

32. The one *least* important would be: ___.

33. The one not listed that should be is: _____.

34. If I were to place *all ten* in priority order, that order would be: ___, ___, ___, ___, ___, ___, ___, ___, ___, ___.

35. The last time I became angry was _____ and it had to do with _____
_____

36. If I discovered tomorrow that I had but one week to live, I would be
   _____ (a) satisfied with my life and the way it has gone
   _____ (b) extremely satisfied with my life
   _____ (c) disappointed at the way things have gone so far and upset that I didn't have any time to make it better

37. When I was in high school I thought of myself as
    (Select those answers that apply to you)
    _____ (a) a winner
    _____ (b) an also-ran
    _____ (c) wanted by others
    _____ (d) shunned by others
    _____ (e) smart; an intellectual leader
    _____ (f) being of average intelligence
    _____ (g) being a bit below average in most areas
    _____ (h) popular
    _____ (i) likeable
    _____ (j) sexy
    _____ (k) beautiful
    _____ (l) handsome
    _____ (m) a loner
    _____ (n) always smiling
    _____ (o) usually smiling
    _____ (p) seldom smiling
    _____ (q) usually growling
    _____ (r) outgoing
    _____ (s) introverted

38. When people meet me, they like me instantly.
    TRUE or FALSE

39. It takes a little while to really get to know me.
    TRUE or FALSE

40. In first contacts with people, I usually put my best foot forward.
    TRUE or FALSE

41. In first contacts with people, I never put my best foot forward. Rather, I present myself more-or-less on a "this is how it is/take it or leave it" basis.
    TRUE or FALSE

42. Right now, I think of myself as
_____ (a) a winner
_____ (b) an also-ran
_____ (c) wanted by others
_____ (d) shunned by others
_____ (e) smart; an intellectual leader
_____ (f) being of average intelligence
_____ (g) being a bit below average in most areas
_____ (h) popular
_____ (i) likeable
_____ (j) sexy
_____ (k) beautiful
_____ (l) handsome
_____ (m) a loner
_____ (n) always smiling
_____ (o) usually smiling
_____ (p) seldom smiling
_____ (q) usually growling
_____ (r) outgoing
_____ (s) introverted

43. If I had to guess, I would say other people see me as
_____ (a) being extremely happy
_____ (b) a friend in need and a friend indeed
_____ (c) usually broke
_____ (d) seldom, if ever, broke
_____ (e) intensely interested in life and all its aspects
_____ (f) a nice but rather bland person
_____ (g) seductive
_____ (h) seduceable
_____ (i) well dressed
_____ (j) slim
_____ (k) fat
_____ (l) having a good body they would like to jump on
_____ (m) generous with money

_____ (n) generous with my time
_____ (o) satisfied with my position in life
_____ (p) a bit dissatisfied
_____ (q) happy to be with my mate
_____ (r) unhappy with my mate but hanging in there to
            see if we can't make it better
_____ (s) someone to go to the ball game with
_____ (t) someone to go to a concert with
_____ (u) someone to go to a lecture with
_____ (v) someone to go to church with
_____ (w) someone to go to bed with
_____ (x) someone they want to go to hell
_____ (y) someone they want to hug and smooch
_____ (z) someone whose hand they want to shake

44. With regard to how I think other people perceive me,
(indicated above), I usually find it is
_____ (a) exactly as I perceive myself
_____ (b) not exactly as I perceive myself

45. If I had to use the same list in Question 43 to indicate my
self-perceptions, I would check off letters:
A B C D E F G H I J K L M N O P Q R S T U V W X Y Z

46. When I am with my lover I know he/she adores me and
loves every minute we are together.
TRUE or FALSE

47. The things I like most about my physical self are
(Select only those that apply)
_____ (a) my eyes
_____ (b) my hands
_____ (c) my legs
_____ (d) my hair
_____ (e) my breasts
_____ (f) my penis
_____ (g) my waistline
_____ (h) my smile

_____ (i) my dimples
_____ (j) my vagina
_____ (k) my feet
_____ (l) my hips
_____ (m) my nose
_____ (n) my cute little behind
_____ (o) my great big behind
_____ (p) my teeth
_____ (q) my ears
_____ (r) my knees
_____ (s) my mouth

48. What other people like most about my body are
A B C D E F G H I J K L M N O P Q R S

49. In bed I am
_____ (a) outrageous
_____ (b) warm and cuddly
_____ (c) daring and inventive
_____ (d) sweet and loving
_____ (e) usually tired
_____ (f) usually excited to be there
_____ (g) shy and demure
_____ (h) outgoing and demonstrative
_____ (i) aggressive
_____ (j) passive
_____ (k) frustrated more often than not
_____ (l) always satisfied
_____ (m) usually satisified
_____ (n) not concerned with being satisfied

50. At work I am
_____ (a) a person to be reckoned with
_____ (b) just another employee
_____ (c) aiming for the top and moving fast
_____ (d) waiting for the day I can get out
_____ (e) always asked my opinion

____ (f)   seldom consulted
____ (g)   the best at what I do
____ (h)   no better nor worse than anybody else
____ (i)   liked by my fellow employees
____ (j)   always on the go
____ (k)   not always understood in terms of my motive or
            intentions
____ (l)   excited to start a new day on the job
____ (m) paid in good proportion to the work I do
____ (n)   paid out of proportion to my work and talents
            ____ overpaid
            ____ underpaid

51. If I found I did not like my job, I would quit my job
tomorrow.
    TRUE or FALSE

52. I would stay at my job no matter what, because I need it to
survive.
    TRUE or FALSE

53. People should be happy they have work and not ask for the
moon.
    TRUE or FALSE

54. People should ask for the moon and refuse to take or keep
any job that is not their highest expression of Self.
    TRUE or FALSE

55. Most people I know are happy in their primary love
relationship.
    TRUE or FALSE

56. I am happy in my primary love relationship
    ____ (a)   all the time
    ____ (b)   almost all the time
    ____ (c)   most of the time
    ____ (d)   enough of the time
    ____ (e)   half of the time

_____ (f)   not enough of the time

_____ (g)   almost none of the time

_____ (h)   none of the time

57. My communication with my spouse or mate is

_____ (a)   exceptional

_____ (b)   usually quite good

_____ (c)   okay

_____ (d)   not always effective

_____ (e)   usually difficult at best

_____ (f)   horrible

58. God, to me, is

_____ (a)   an unproven concept

_____ (b)   a living presence in my life

_____ (c)   a thing of which I am a part

_____ (d)   the most powerful force in the universe

_____ (e)   a hazy concept I can't really get in touch with but somehow feel is real at some level

_____ (f)   a person, force, or entity I can get in touch with at the drop of a hat

_____ (g)   my best friend

_____ (h)   my Self

59. If we do not do good or if we harm other people, we will all go to hell.
     TRUE or FALSE

60. We won't go to hell no matter what we do, because there is no hell.
     TRUE or FALSE

61. When I die, I will

_____ (a)   continue to exist in another realm

_____ (b)   go straight to hell

_____ (c)   discontinue conscious awareness

_____ (d)   sit at the right hand of God the Father Almighty

_____ (e)   be happy

_____ (f)   have to reconcile myself with my sins

_____ (g)   see what I've learned and have a chance to do this all over again

_____ (h)   The question is irrelevant because I am not going to die.

_____ (i)   Don't know.

62. If I were to have to judge myself and the way I have lived my life right now, I would say

_____ (a)   I have sinned.

_____ (b)   I accept myself without judgment.

_____ (c)   I never committed a sin in my life.

_____ (d)   I committed a few, but I'm okay now.

63. On a Goodness Scale of 10, I am a _____.

64. If I found myself with 200 people on an all-nude beach right now I would

_____ (a)   be embarrassed and find a place to hide

_____ (b)   be delighted and find a place to strut

_____ (c)   be surprised and find a place to smile and watch

_____ (d)   be shocked and find a place to run

_____ (e)   have no problem with it at all

_____ (f)   wish I wasn't there

65. What bothers me the most about the world as it is today is

_____

_____

_____

66. What I love most about the world today is

_____

_____

_____

67. If I could be anything I wanted to be, I would be

_____

68. If I could do anything I wanted to do, I would

_____

69. If I could have anything I wanted to have, I would have

_____

70. Of the above three things,   ALL   ONE   TWO   *(circle the correct answer)* are what is happening in my life right now.

71. This has been a fascinating questionnaire and I had fun answering the questions.
TRUE or FALSE

72. I feel good about all of my answers and wouldn't change a thing—that is, I am glad that I could honestly answer every one of the questions as I did.
TRUE or FALSE

73. I wish I could have answered some questions differently and still be honest.
TRUE or FALSE

74. I am going to pass this instrument on to a friend. I am dying to see *their* answers.
TRUE or FALSE

75. Now, having finished this questionnaire, on a scale of 10 I would rate my present state of life a _____.

76. The above is
    _____ (a)   okay with me
    _____ (b)   not okay with me, but I don't seem to be able to do anything about it
    _____ (c)   not okay with me, and I am going to change it

• • •

Congratulations! You've just finished the questionnaire! Now if you want to do something *really* daring, invite someone else to take part in this process with you. By following the instructions below, you will be able to widen the scope of your personal inquiry and broaden this part of the Divine Experiment to include those closest to you.

You can do this and maintain the total privacy of your answers to the above questionnaire, or you may share your responses with another—as you wish.

Do you have a person or persons with whom you feel safe enough to share all of the responses you gave to the questions above? If not, you may still share the process by sharing the questions but not revealing your *answers* to anyone.

Perception Check

This is a perception check. Follow these instructions carefully, and you will discover
- (a) how you perceive life and yourself
- (b) how other people think you perceive yourself (in other words, how accurately you project your true Self)
- (c) how other people perceive you
- (d) that items B and C do not matter

1. Go back and reread your answers to this questionnaire. See and hear what you have just said to yourself about how it really is for you in all of the above areas. Decide what these answers mean to you. (Even deciding it means nothing is okay.)

2. Give this questionnaire to a spouse, mate, or friend. Ask that person to fill out the questionnaire as *they think you would fill it out.* To find out how they think you perceive yourself, check the answers they predicted you would give against those you actually gave. This is an excellent way to see if the "you" you project is the "you" you feel inside.

You do not have to show your answers to your partner unless you wish to. If you wish to keep them private, tell your partner ahead of time that you would like him or her to take part in an experiment with you, but he or she has to be willing not to see the results.

3. While you are checking their guesses as to how you would answer against your actual answers, give them another copy of the questionnaire and ask them to fill it out as they see you. Now you can check the perception others have of you.

Now, if you like and if your partner is willing, you may reverse the process. Ask your partner to give his or her *own* answers to the questionnaire. Meanwhile, you answer the questionnaire (a) as you think they will answer (i.e., as you think they see themselves) and (b) as you see them.

Now you have done a good day's work, but you are not through—unless you want to be. (Nobody gets to tell you what to do!)

To sort out and get clear your reactions to the above process, do the following short exercise.

Clearing Process

1. Take out a sheet of paper and write out your initial reactions to what you have just done.

2. Take out a second sheet and mark it TO BE USED IN 48 HOURS. Put it on your dresser, refrigerator, bathroom mirror—someplace where you can't forget to get back to it in two days. The day after tomorrow, after two days of thinking about it and just being with it, take this sheet and write out your reactions to what you did today.

3. Complete the following statements on the experiment:

• What interested me most about this process was _____
_____

• What made me happiest was _____
_____

- What I have decided about my life, if anything, as a result of this process is _____
_____

This is exciting. Now we are rolling. Now we are on our way along the Inner Path. This is only the beginning. The next part of the experiment is taking your place as my coauthor in this book. When you are ready to do that, go to the next page.

Do not be nervous about the next chapter. It really is going to be the most interesting chapter in the book. I will help you write it, giving you hints along the way. It will be the first chapter of *Your New Story*. You will be writing the remaining chapters in the days and weeks and months and years ahead.

With this book, you officially become the author of your life story. You write the script, you determine the plot, you decide how it all goes. With your participation as a coauthor of the book you are holding in your hands, you take in your hands the power to continue being the author of every chapter to follow. You are, in short, *author-izing* an experience called life, rather than simply having it.

When you are ready to take control, be your own ideal, and move to mastery in life . . . *turn to the next chapter!*

⚹⚹⚹

17. The Greatest Story Ever Told: Yours!

Take out your notebook and at the top on the first page write the words *The Inner Path, Chapter 17: The Greatest Story Ever Told.*

Now write this chapter, copying out of this book, as you come to them, the lead-in sentences that follow to give you a little help. This is not just an "exercise." It is an important part of your completion of this book. I am asking you to write the next chapter right now. You will find this is not only the most interesting but the most important part of the book.

Please copy the story line below into your notebook, filling in the blanks as you go.

• • •

ONCE UPON A TIME, in a land not so very far away, there lived a person named _____.
I am that person and this is my story.

Most of this story has to do with my future, because that is

215

where the action is, that is where the excitement is, and that is where the happiness, satisfaction, and fulfillment are.

Still, a little about my past might be useful in placing this wonderful story into context.

I was born on _____, 19_____, in _____, _____, making me _____ years old as I write this story. My mother's name was _____, and my father's name was _____. (NOTE: *Some people will have to write "not known to me" for one or both of the above.*) I have _____ brothers and _____ sisters.

As a child I was _____
_____
_____
_____
_____
_____

My fondest childhood memory is of the time when _____
_____
_____
_____
_____
_____
_____
_____
_____
_____
_____
_____
_____
_____
_____
_____

If I could say there was one thing I learned from this experience that I use today in my day-to-day life, it would be that _____

_____

_____

_____

_____

_____

_____

_____

_____

_____

Lots of special things happened to me when I was little. For instance, one of the most special gifts I ever received was _____

_____

_____

and a neat thing I once won was _____

_____

_____.

But the most wonderful thing of all about my childhood was

_____

_____.

Time flew by, and soon I was attending _____
_____ High School in _____.
My best friend in school was _____ and we spent a lot of time together. My most successful high school experience involved the time that I _____

_____

_____.

From my teenage years to young adulthood now seems like an instant jump. And from that time to this feels even less than instant, if that is possible. Yet there have been some experiences in between with major impact on my life. One of the best of these was _____

_____
_____
_____
_____
_____
_____
_____
_____.

Others include _____

_____
_____

and _____

_____
_____.

Life, of course, has always been a challenge. Without its challenge, it would scarcely have a purpose. The biggest problem I ever overcame in my life was _____.

Now I am preparing to embark on the rest of my life. I know what I want to see clearly in my future. This is the story of what that future will be.

To begin with, my life will be a great adventure. It will be neither boring nor without direction and purpose. And while everything that has gone on in my life up until now has prepared me for this moment, my life in the future will have nothing to do with my past. All of the limiting beliefs that I have had in the past will be dropped, and I will live in the moment from my experience.

Three past beliefs that I now clearly can see no longer serve me, and which will be eliminated, are the beliefs that

1. _____
2. _____
3. _____

My life will be newly energized and injected with a sense of

purpose, a reason for living. From this time forward the
purpose of my life will be _____
_____
_____.

Everything I choose to be, do, and have will serve this
purpose. I am excited now to be able to describe some of these
things for you. I am very clear on these things, and visualize
them with remarkable detail. It is as if it is all happening right
now.

For instance, I have my perfect relationship, and my partner
is _____
_____
_____.

My life work is totally exciting, totally rewarding, and
totally fulfilling. I am _____
_____
_____.

My income is perfect for my needs. I receive $ _____ a
year.

I am at my perfect weight of _____ pounds and my
appearance and wardrobe are wonderful!

I am paying loving attention to myself and part of that is
being selective about what I eat. Here is my usual daily diet:
_____
_____
_____
_____
_____
_____
_____.

Three other things I do every day to love myself are
1. _____
2. _____
3. _____

My living quarters are the most comfortable and the most "me" I have ever created. Let me describe them to you.

_____

_____

_____

_____

_____

_____

_____

_____

_____.

My life is one of accomplishment, fulfillment, and achievement. A major goal I have realized is _____

_____.

The contributions I make to people's lives make a difference. My most significant contribution is _____

_____

_____.

I have become a dynamic, loving, caring human being with a positive impact on others. When people meet me they say that I am unforgettable, and the thing they remember most about me is _____

_____.

In short, this life is turning out to be the highest expression of my Self I ever imagined! But what I have written thus far describes only the physical aspects of it. I have also reached a new level of mastery in experiencing the mental, emotional, and spiritual parts of my being.

I am free of fear, doubts, guilt, recrimination, nervousness about my future, worry about how it will look to others, or concern for whether or not I am approved of, accepted, or rejected.

My state of mind is _____, my emotional state is _____, and

for me the highest spiritual truth is that I am _____
_____.

This is how I choose to create my tomorrow. Besides what I have mentioned above, my life will be distinguished by

_____

_____

_____

_____

_____

_____

_____.

I realize that I can create life the way I want it, and this is the way I want it. In this new and perfect expression of Self which makes up my life adventure, I find that I am happiest when I

_____

_____,

I am wisest when I _____
_____,

I am most loving when I _____
_____.

This is the way it is for me now that I have embarked on the Adventure of the Soul, undertaken the Divine Experiment, and chosen to walk the Inner Path.

The remaining chapters in The Greatest Story Ever Told—
my story—are yet to be written. I will write them. As the author of my life, I realize that This Moment is, always has been, and always will be . . .

THE BEGINNING

✿✿✿

Epilogue:
An Opening Word

Speak the truth.
Give whatever you can,
never be angry.
These three steps will lead you
into the presence of the gods.

The Dhammapada
(The Sayings of the Buddha)

O NCE UPON A TIME, in a land not very far away, there lived
a little girl named Terry. She wanted nothing more than
to love people and be happy—and be loved back, of course,
which she *knew* would make her happy.

This little girl had a Momma and a Poppa and a Nanny and a
Grampa George and three wonderful siblings and, and . . .

• • •

I could spend all day telling you my story in even greater
detail than I've shared with you already, but I am sure you
have just learned that yours is far more interesting.

If your life story has not been all that wonderful up to now,
then you are in the same position I was in back in La Cañada,
and you have to ask yourself the same questions I asked myself
then. How much more dullness and depression will you have
to endure? How many more "takes" must there be of this film
of futility and frustration? Are you to suffer through not only
a summer but a lifetime of reruns?

The good news is that you can bring down the curtain, and you can do it right now. This doesn't mean you have to get out of the acting business. (You couldn't if you wanted to.) It simply means you can go on to another show.

Whether you want to or not is another matter. Only you can know for sure. Some people like their tragedies. They wouldn't give them up for the world.

Only you can know whether you've had enough pain, enough frustration, enough sadness, enough loneliness and depression, enough fear and guilt and failure. Only you can know for sure, but I think playwright and author Patrick Dennis summed up the general state of the human condition fairly well in the scintillating line he wrote for his wonderfully scintillating Broadway play, *Auntie Mame:* "Life is a banquet and most poor sons-of-bitches are starving to death!"

• • •

The idea behind the sharing in this book has not been that my truths will become your truths, but that mine might lead you to yours. I do not have your answers, but I have had some of your questions.

Both of us at this moment are conducting a divine experiment. You may call it simply "life," but it is the same process, the same activity. It doesn't matter what you call it. You can't get out of it, you can't not do it. It is exactly as I said earlier: "The function of life is to feel. You can feel whatever you choose, but *you can't choose not to feel anything.*"

You now get to decide what you want to feel for the rest of your life. It will not be an easy decision if, like most of us, you are deeply attached to your dramas. Without drama and pain it may seem for a while as though you are not alive, as though you are walking around in a trance. This is because we associate pain with life, and release and bliss with death. When we experience release and bliss in life it seems unnatural. Yet nothing in the world could be *more* natural. The state of bliss is the natural state; the state of pain is unnatural.

You get to choose right now which path you will take, the outer path of the world as you see it, or the Inner Path into a world of your own creation. You may opt to stick with what you have called real life, or you may choose to be a modern-day Don Quixote, imagining all taverns to be castles, all ladies to be fair, all men to be honorable, all rags to be silk, and all life to be magic.

You may choose to dream the seemingly impossible dream.

What you choose will not matter to anyone, least of all to God. God allows. God does not judge, God does not get damaged, God does not go off in a corner and huff and puff and blow the house down to show you who is boss. God allows. God allows because God is That Which Includes All. God allows because God is not a being, God is That Which Includes All Beings. God is the All of it and the Everything, and God cannot be apart from any of it in any way.

What you choose will matter only to you, and only to the degree that you care who you are.

As for me, I already know who you are. I see who you are and I acknowledge you in all your holiness, in all your magnificence, in all your power and glory and splendor. I see who you are, and I thank you for allowing me the opportunity to share with you who I am.

Whatever choice you make,

I love you,

Terry

Appendix:
Exercises and Affirmations

The exercises and affirmations that follow are designed to be undertaken after reading the chapters to which they relate. Do not attempt to do these exercises ahead of time or out of sequence.

The exercises will in many cases require you to write, so be ready with a pen or pencil and paper or your notebook. (A notebook, rather than loose sheets, is suggested, so that you can keep the material together in one place for easy review.)

You will also need the notebook for the affirmations assigned to each chapter.

Affirmations are statements that affirm the truth of your own experience. They are not tools with which you produce a specific outcome (as many people mistakenly believe), but descriptions of outcomes that already have been produced. When used in the first context, they rarely prove to be a satisfactory expenditure of time and nearly always bring disappointment. When used in the second way, they are the most powerful statements on earth.

Christ did not say to the man who came to him, "Your

daughter is not dead, she merely sleeps" as a statement of what he *hoped would happen*, but as a statement of what he *knew to be so*, even though he had no physical evidence before him to support his bold, seemingly preposterous statement. This is how you should use affirmations. Christ simply affirmed the truth with every word he spoke, with every thought he formed. He also made it clear that he was not any more special in his abilities than any of us. Note his remark: "Why are you so amazed? These things and more shall you also do."

Now it is your turn to use the power of your word to affirm the truth. When using affirmations for the first time, it is best to write them out in longhand rather than simply to repeat them silently or out loud, as writing embeds them in your mind—in your awareness. You may create your own affirmations on any subject, of course. There is no "correct" way to create them, but here are some tips that will make them very powerful.

- Always state affirmations in the present tense, as something that is happening or that is true for you *right now.*
- Do not begin with affirmations that are beyond your ability to embrace—for example, "I have five million dollars in cash right now." (Not that such a miracle is not possible, because it is, of course. In fact, to God such an event would be quite trivial.) Your mind will automatically limit you to what you can sincerely believe. So allow your first affirmations to be wholly within your grasp, wholly acceptable to even your "doubting Thomas" logical mind. An example of a first affirmation might be, "My financial good is coming to me now and every day, bringing me closer and closer to my highest abundance and prosperity."
- Use affirmations regularly. Do not use them now and then, only to stop for weeks or months on end until the next time you feel you need one. That is how most people pray, and it is one reason most people find prayer unsatisfactory.
- Eventually graduate your affirmations from the written

word to the spoken and then the thought-of word. That is, let every thought, word, and deed ultimately be an affirmation of what is true about you and life. (In fact, this is what is going on right now. Observe your present thoughts, words, and actions and you will find your present life is a direct reflection of them!)

A series of affirmations follows the exercises for each of the indicated chapters. When writing these in your notebook, insert your name or the names of others where appropriate.

Exercises and Affirmations for
Chapter 10: Blockages to the Vision

The four exercises that follow have been designed to assist you in discovering and eliminating behavior patterns that you no longer want in your life and in removing the blockages you may have to living your highest vision.

Begin by taking out your notebook and making some observations about your life. Make a list of the things that seem to recur:

- The same situations
- The same types of relationships
- The same results
- The same job situations
- The same health conditions
- Whatever else repeats in your life

1. Note your thoughts, beliefs, attitudes, body conditions, etc., that echo those of your parents and family. List as many as you can identify. (Examples: "All good things come to an end"; "My father was heavy-set, so it is okay for me to be fat"; "Every time I meet someone I really like, they don't like me"; "My father was the dominant one in our family relationship, and my husband is now the dominant one in mine"; and

so forth, listing any repeating pattern that you can trace to your parents and family.)

(a) Be aware of what you are repeating when you feel like a victim and when you feel hopeless because "it happened again." Write out as many of these instances as you can remember now, and be conscious of them in the future. (Examples: "My lover left me holding the bag again"; "Someone else at work got the credit one more time for something I did"; "My brother won the argument *AGAIN*"; "I got taken to the cleaners financially by my family one more time"; "My business partners are cheating me again"; "My spouse always gets her/his way, and I always give in to what he/she wants.")

(b) Look at each pattern that has developed. Ask yourself, Does this pattern serve me or limit me? Examine the value you receive from each pattern and then simply choose whether you wish to continue that behavior.

2. Observe yourself as you interact with people tomorrow. Listen to the words you speak, notice the feelings you allow yourself, see the situations in which you find yourself, watch how you relate to people, mentally summarize any "battles" you are fighting—or resisting. Notice that it all is *your* creation!

(a) Tomorrow evening, come back to your notebook and make a list of judgments that you have placed on yourself and others concerning the above. Notice how many times condemnation causes you to *repeat* a situation.

(b) Decide to break the pattern by loving yourself and others enough to allow yourself to be just the way you are and everybody else to be just the way they are.

Here is an interesting optional exercise to go along with the above. List the times you can remember in the past month, year, and five years when it was not okay with you that someone important or close to you held an opinion or point of view concerning an issue you cared about that was not in concert with your own. Now go over the list and make a note next to each incident indicating what difference it makes today that this division occurred. Probably not a great deal! Observe what this tells you about becoming upset when someone has a truth different from yours.

3. To free yourself of money problems that cause you to block your own vision and feel trapped and helpless, do this exercise:
  (a) Write out twenty-five fears, conflicts, or thoughts you have about your being rich, wealthy, and able to do as you choose and have what you desire.
  (b) Take out your notebook or a sheet of paper and write across the top of the page, "What payoff or value do I receive from making money a problem and denying myself what I want?" Answer the question in as much detail as possible.

4. Think about your vision, forgetting any past patterns or present blockages, and then feel yourself being, doing, and having your ideal.
  (a) Keep a journal or diary of your reaction to how you feel. (Be sure to make an entry each day.) Notice if any blockages come up ("This feels silly," or, "I'm too old to play pretend"), and notice also if your experience of life during these "make-believe minutes" is any different from your experience the rest of the day.

Affirmations

Here are the affirmations for Chapter 10. Write each of them twenty times each day until you have the experience of their truth. This may seem like a lot of writing, but do it anyway. It actually will only take you a matter of minutes, and it could change your life.

I, _____, no longer need to be loyal to *(name of person)* by taking on their thoughts, patterns, or life-style.

I, _____, give myself permission to be abundant and prosperous.

I, _____, no longer believe in success or failure, only in doing what I want that makes me happy.

I, _____, now break all agreements within my soul-memory that have kept me limited in any way.

I, _____, now live my life for myself from love, joy, and a sense of adventure.

The more I contemplate love, the more love I experience.

The more I contemplate what I desire, the more I have what I want.

I, _____, break all past agreements that have kept me in guilt, fear, pain, poverty, or unhappiness.

I, _____, am free to be my joyous and glorious self.

Exercises and Affirmations for
Chapter 11: Giving/Receiving

The four exercises that follow should be undertaken only after reading Chapter 11. (Please do not participate in the exercises found in this appendix out of sequence.)

The exercises and affirmations here deal with giving and receiving, which is Step One on the Inner Path.

1. Feel yourself receiving and having just what you desire. Imagine, sense, and experience yourself as receiving whatever you want.

2. In your notebook, write out twenty-five energy blockages (fears or conflicts) you can sense yourself having to your receiving everything you want all the time. (For example: "If I have all the sex I want, I will not be okay with God"; "I cannot be trusted with more money than I could imagine"; "Money

and spirituality don't mix"; "I cannot have too much power within my company or organization because I will then be vulnerable and will get hurt"; "Getting all the attention I'd really like to have would be unacceptable. I am to be seen and not heard"; "If I had too much, others would try to take it away from me"; "The higher they go, the harder they fall"; "Don't rock the boat and nobody'll get hurt"; "Nice guys finish last"; "You can't fight City Hall"; "Nobody likes me when they think I'm better than they are in any way"; etc.)

    (a) Write out your payoff, or the value you get, from depriving yourself and denying yourself freedom of expression.

    (b) Write a statement of what it costs you to deny yourself life.

    (c) Make a list of the benefits you think you would receive from having no fear of giving or receiving.

3. Practice giving compliments, acknowledgment, and support to others. Go past your fear of others being, doing, and having more than you. Realize that no one can take anything away from you and that the more you desire others to be all that they are, the more you receive this same fullness for yourself.

4. Make a list of five things, material or nonmaterial (money, love, etc.), that you do not think you have enough of. Find a way to give away some of each of these things in the next twenty-four hours. Each time you give, breathe deeply and affirm, "Every gift I give is returned to me multiplied." Repeat the exercise every other day for a week. After two weeks off, do the exercise again.

Affirmations

Write out each affirmation twenty times per day, and allow yourself to feel the statement is already true.

I, _____, give everyone the freedom to live as they choose.

The more I give, the more I receive, and I now receive my kingdom and treasure.

I, _____, now feel alive, wealthy, loving, and whole.

I, _____, give to myself all I desire to feel, do, and have. I am unlimited forever.

It's okay for me to give love and acceptance to others because it comes back to me multiplied one hundred times.

I, _____, am worthy and deserving of all of God's treasure, love, and happiness.

I am abundant in all I desire, and I affirm my having by giving. Each time I give _____ I receive _____.

Exercises and Affirmations for
Chapter 12: Forgiveness

1. Take out your notebook and make a list of the people with whom you are upset, angry, resentful, dissapointed, or unhappy. Write next to each name what that person did or didn't do that upset you.

   (a) Experience the feeling or emotion that you expected but did not receive in each interaction (love, respect, happiness, joy, peace, self-acceptance, equality, beauty, wealth, power, security, etc.). Then ask yourself why you need to forgive anyone for not "giving you" that when *you* could give yourself the feeling you want any time.

   (b) Next to each name on your "offender's list," make a notation of the payoff you received in each instance out of resentment, blame, and judgment.

   (c) Now write down what you have *not* received—what it cost you to hold onto resentment, the past, hurt, pain, and self-pity.

2. On a separate page, write out a short scenario of what you would be doing, how you would be living, what you would have, and how you would feel if you were free of blame, resentment, and self-pity.

   (a) Make a list of everything you would love to be, do, and have right now.

   (b) Spend time each day loving and releasing those you have not forgiven; see, sense, and feel them being totally happy, abundant, loving, healthy, and joyful. (You can only have what you are willing to see others have.)

3. Envision life as a film and everyone as actors, directors, writers, producers, and audience. See yourself as one who has merely been playing a part in a drama that you created to gain wisdom and the experience. See if you can get in touch with the fact that nothing means anything, that it was all a stage show for the joy and fun of it. Release yourself and others from the grip of meaning, and set yourself free to live *as spirit* once again. Acknowledge yourself and everyone for parts well played.

Spend time each day in a peaceful and beautiful setting where you can release the part you have been playing; allow yourself to be lifted into a faster vibration or frequency of energy by loving yourself, feeling peaceful, and feeling unlimited. The more you feel this way, the more joyful your life will be.

4. If you find yourself judging another or yourself, say to yourself, "All judgment is meaningless, and I now acknowledge the love that I am and that they are."

Affirmations

Write each of the following affirmations in your notebook twenty times each day until you feel the statement to be true and real for you. Feeling is the desired result.

I, _____, joyously acknowledge the gift I have received from _____'s *(name a person with whom you have had a disagreement)* being in my life.

I, _____, have always had the choice to live as I choose and I always will.

I, _____, now release _____ *(name of person)* from any blame and bless them in all they desire for themselves.

I, _____, release myself from the bondage of resentment and free myself to live my own truth and be my own ideal.

I, _____, no longer limit myself by judging, condemning, or blaming _____ *(name of person with whom you have had a disagreement)*. He/she is my mirror and I love her/him.

From the Lord God of my Totality my soul will release all blame, resentment, and judgment from my energy so that I am free to be fully me.

Added Power-Packed Exercise

Take ten to twenty minutes out of each day to feel as you would if there were no one stopping or resisting you and you were 100 percent unlimited and could be and create anything you desire.

Feel yourself uplifted into a greater realm of non-judgment, where you allow everyone, including yourself, to be as he or she is, knowing each of us creates what we desire for ourselves. Feel unlimited.

Exercises and Affirmations for
Chapter 13: Guiltlessness

Achieving and experiencing a state of guiltlessness is the third step on the Inner Path. The following exercises and affirmations will assist you in moving into this state.

1. Each morning for the next week look into a mirror for fifteen minutes and love, admire, bless, and honor yourself by feeling love and appreciation for you and the glorious Creator.

    (a) Any thoughts or feelings of judgment, guilt, or self-pity, that occur are part of the cleansing process. *Feel them* and allow them to pass by saying, "Everything I did I needed to do for the wisdom of the experience. I love and acknowledge myself for my courage to be."

    (b) As you bless yourself each day at the mirror, ask yourself what you can do this day that will bring you more glory, more joy, and more happiness.

2. Make a list of everything about which you feel guilty. Notice what your *good* intentions were behind those actions. Realize what you learned, then burn the paper.

3. Write a note to or telephone each person about whom you have a feeling of guilt and ask their forgiveness for whatever it is that causes you to feel guilty around them. Free yourself by realizing what it is you did or didn't do that you judged, and actively choose to "play guilt" no longer.

4. If you notice others trying to use guilt on you—or yourself using it on another—simply love yourself and them and don't play the game. Remember, it is your life and you were not born to live someone else's dream nor to be what someone else wants you to be. *Live for yourself* from love and joy and notice then that all are served in the highest way.

    (a) Make a list in your notebook of ways that you can remember serving others in the highest way, doing exactly what you wanted and being exactly who you were. Love yourself for this.

(b) Make a list in your notebook of the times you felt you had to be or do something other than what the "real you" would be or do and this backfired, giving the person or organization you were trying to please a "loss" rather than a "win."

(c) Notice how being less than you or other than you cheats not only you but everyone else.

Affirmations

Write each of the following affirmations in your notebook twenty times each day until you feel each statement to be true and real for you.

From the Lord God of my Being I lovingly command my soul to no longer acknowledge guilt, and I remove guilt from my vibration. So be it.

I, _____, can trust myself without using guilt.

I, _____, now release myself from social consciousness and the realm of guilt. I am free.

I, _____, rejoice in others' living as they choose, just as I rejoice in my living as I choose.

I, _____, no longer control myself or (name of another) with guilt.

I, _____, acknowledge myself for being the great creator that I am, and I align myself with all people at the level of a higher truth for all.

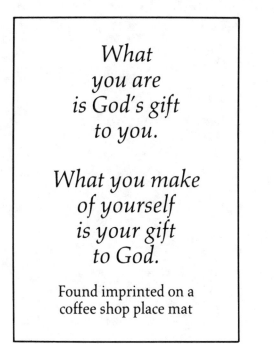

*What
you are
is God's gift
to you.*

*What you make
of yourself
is your gift
to God.*

Found imprinted on a
coffee shop place mat